The Street-wise Popular Practical Guides

"A fantastic book that not only provides a comprehensive overview of the law, but crucially empowers individuals to have a better understanding of the legal industry so that they understand their options when engaging a legal professional."
– **James Antoniou,** Solicitor, Head of Practice, *Co-Op Legal Services.*

The Street-wise Popular Practical Guides

EER Street-wise Guides No. 4.

The Street-wise Guide To Getting The Best From Your Lawyer

Gill Steel

EER

Edward Everett Root, Publishers, Brighton, 2018.

EER

Edward Everett Root, Publishers, Co. Ltd.,
30 New Road, Brighton, Sussex, BN1 1BN, England.
www.eerpublishing.com

edwardeverettroot@yahoo.co.uk

Gill Steel

The Street-wise Guide To Getting the Best From Your Lawyer

First published in Great Britain in 2018.

The Street-wise Popular Practical Guides, no.4.

ISBN: 978-1-912224-62-3 paperback.
ISBN: 978-1-912224-63-0 hardback.
ISBN: 978-1-912224-64-7 ebook.

Typeset in Book Antiqua

Designed by Pageset Limited, High Wycombe, Buckinghamshire.
Printed and bound by Lightning Source UK, Milton Keynes.

The Street-wise Popular Practical Guides

Edited by Karol Sikora and John Spiers.

This original paperback series provides *practical,* expert, insider-knowledge.

Each book tells you what professionals know, but which is not often shared with the public at large.

The books provide vital insider guidance, including what some authorities would prefer you never to know.

The authors are all internationally acknowledged professional experts and skilled popular writers.

We will be pleased to receive suggestions for other titles.

AVAILABLE.
Robert Lefever, *The Street-wise Guide to Coping with and Recovering from Addiction.*

Karol Sikora, *The Street-wise Patient's Guide To Surviving Cancer. How to be an active, organised, informed, and welcomed patient.*

Lady Teviot, *The Street-wise Guide to Doing Your Family History.*

FORTHCOMING.
Tom Balchin, *The Street-wise Guide to Surviving a Stroke.*

Georgina Burnett, *The Street-wise Guide to Buying, Improving, and Selling Your Home.*

Eamonn Butler, *The Street-wise Guide to the UK Economy: The Politics of Britain's Present and Future.*

Sam Collins, *The Street-wise Guide to Choosing a Care Home.*

Stephen Davies, *The Street-wise Guide to the Devil and His Works.*

Raj Persaud and Peter Bruggen, *The Street-wise Guide to Getting the Best Mental Health Care. How to Survive the Mental Health System and Get Some Proper Help.*

Nung Rudarakanchana, *The Street-wise Woman's Guide to Getting The Best Healthcare.*

For John, Jack and Audrey

Contents

About the author

Gill Steel, LLB, ATT, TEP, MBA, is a solicitor who has operated in the field of legal training and consulting for over 20 years. She has more than 30 years specialist experience in Wills, Probate, Trusts Tax and Elderly Client issues. She also provides off-the-shelf or bespoke training for organisations and professional bodies. As this book shows, Gill has a gift for making Wills, Probate, Trusts, Tax and Elderly Client topics practical, engaging, informative and clear.

An extremely knowledgeable and inspirational conference speaker, Gill is known by thousands of private client practitioners and has spoken at over 900 events with regular engagements throughout the country. She has an MBA in Legal Practice, and is the author of *The Trust Practitioner's Handbook* (currently on its 3rd edition) published by The Law Society and Consultant Editor on *Tolley's IHT Trusts & Estates Guidance*. Gill is a member of the Society of Trust and Estate Practitioners (STEP) UK Practice Committee and the Association of Taxation Technicians.

Acknowledgements

Whilst the law and practice mentioned in this book is my responsibility and is stated as at 1 February 2018 I could not have produced this book without the help of my Editor, John Spiers and the following people: my husband for his practical help from practising law for over 45 years; my Executive Assistant Sue Sheppard whose support is tireless and patient; my librarian Helen Wood who keeps me up to date with references and know-how; various colleagues I have shared the idea with, and whose contributions have been quoted in the text, who have given their time to being interviewed or reading the text; and to the many members of the public who read my website and raise questions which demonstrate the complexity of finding a legal solution for people who are not lawyers but must use the law to gain re-dress. This book is for them and everyone faced with trying to achieve justice and fairness.

Gill Steel, Director, *LawSkills Ltd*

Preface

This book aims to help the consumer find the right lawyer or right approach to their problem. Not all problems are legal and often it is a question of teasing out whether a lawyer is the appropriate person to help or not before you embark on finding the right one.

In writing this text I have drawn on over 30 years professional experience in both acting as a solicitor myself but also in providing learning and development for all sorts of practitioners specifically providing advice about Wills, estate administration, trusts, tax and the law on acting for the elderly and vulnerable client.

My experience has urged me to write a book on how best a street-wise consumer could benefit from the law and from lawyers – from expert solicitors, barristers and specialists in each subject field.

I especially offer important pointers on what to do with regards to the law concerning the key events in life: buying a home; dealing with taxation; getting a divorce; managing succession to a business; writing a Will and handling the estate on death of a relative. I offer guidance on sources of advice, and how to tackle these and other specifics, in each chapter. There is also a checklist for each key area of action.

We all want honest, skilled, reliable and value-for-money advice. We are fortunate in that some legal activities are carefully regulated by official and professional bodies. My purpose is to help the lay person to know the best place to go for the right legal advice and for constructive help.

I have emphasised preparing yourself by reading the relevant section of the book and finding out what kinds of help are available to you. The street-wise reader will not depend on hindsight, but on foresight if possible. I also offer guidance on the kinds of benefits which can be provided by a professional adviser.

The Law is complicated. Despite living on an island and being part of the United Kingdom there are different legal jurisdictions within our land. This book tackles the law in England & Wales because it is what I know but you must realise that there are differences, sometimes significant differences, in not just the law but also the institutions around it and the professional rules for practising it, in Scotland and Northern Ireland.

At one time the whole of the UK was subject to the same tax rules but this is also changing since devolution and both Scotland and Wales have exercised these fiscal powers to charge tax differently.

The Channel Isles and the Isle of Man, whilst close to our shores, have different legal systems and tax systems as well. Each of them are perhaps known as places of low taxation attracting investment from around the globe.

Where the street-wise consumer lives in any part of the United Kingdom other than England & Wales or is concerned about the law in these other parts of the United Kingdom and the Channel Isles you will need to seek either local advice or find a practitioner in England or Wales who might have offices or links with the other jurisdictions. Depending on what your query is many professionals are familiar with dealing with lawyers in other jurisdictions (including outside the United Kingdom) and where necessary could point you in the right direction or make recommendations.

Of course, neither I as the author or my publisher can take any responsibility for actions taken, either by the reader, their family members, or an adviser as a result of reading this book. However, the greatest care has been taken to responsibly provide accurate and up to date information here.

I also offer a descriptive account of the legal structures and the constitutional framework for England and Wales, and indicate where to seek advice concerning the law in Northern Ireland, Scotland and the Channel Isles.

Guide to jargon

Administration of Oaths	An oath is a sworn statement to be relied on in court. To witness a signature on oath requires someone who is authorised to administer oaths. In the context of dealing with the estate of a deceased person a commissioner for oaths, before whom you would swear to the truth of the contents of the document and sign it, can be a court officer at the Probate Registry or a solicitor.
Administrator	The person permitted to deal with the administration of a deceased person's estate where there is no Will or no-one named as executor able or willing to act.
Advance decision	A choice made whilst you are mentally able to make a choice as to the sort of medical procedures you would not want in the event you were unable to give consent or refuse consent at the relevant time.
Alternative Business Structure	A business offering legal services which is not entirely owned by lawyers but which is regulated in a similar way to solicitors.
Ancillary	Matters which flow from the main action such as financial settlement proceedings connected with divorce.
Attorney	A person who is appointed by a person making a power of attorney (the donor) authorising the attorney to make decisions on behalf of the donor.
Beneficiary	A person who benefits from the estate of a deceased person or under the terms of a trust
Capital Assets	For example investments such as shares or property as opposed to your earnings from employment or interest on bank accounts
Certificate Provider	A person who confirms the donor of a Lasting Power of Attorney understood the nature of making the power and did so freely

Chattels	Personal belongings such as art work, jewellery, the contents of your home
Cohabitation agreement	A formal written document entered into by cohabitants to set out the basis on which they will share their finances
Commissioner for Oaths	A person legally permitted to witness the making of an Oath (a sworn statement of the truth) used in obtaining a Grant of representation
Conflict of Interest	Where the best interests of one client would potentially be at odds with another or where the self-interest of a trustee for example would be at odds with the best interests of the beneficiaries
Contentious/ non-contentious	A matter becomes contentious when there is a dispute between different parties involved. So for the most part the administration of a deceased person's estate would be non-contentious and the process for administration will be dealt with as normal. However, if a person challenges the validity of the Will or claims the financial provision for them under the Will is not reasonable the matter now becomes contentious and may have to be resolved by court proceedings
Contract Law	A part of the English legal system dealing with agreements such as a contract to purchase a property or buy goods or services
CoP	Court of Protection
Counselling	Counselling is a talking therapy that involves a trained therapist listening to you and helping you find ways to deal with emotional issues
Covenants	A promise to do something e.g. pay a regular sum of money to someone each year or a restriction on your enjoyment of a property e.g. a restriction on your use of the property which benefits a neighbour

Declaration of Trust	A Deed setting out the terms on which an asset such as a life assurance policy or a property is held e.g. the property may be in the name of one person but the declaration explains they hold the legal title subject to both their own and another person's interest in the proceeds of sale
Deed(s)	A document or documents which formally explain a transaction such as title deeds for a property or trust deeds in relation to a gift to people to manage for others. A deed must be in writing and the signatures of the parties must be witnessed
Deprivation of Liberty	Where an individual is unable to consent to the care provided to them others have to make decisions about that care in their best interests. To ensure their liberty is not wrongly undermined there are safeguards in place to ensure no wrongful deprivation of liberty occurs
Deputy	A person appointed by the Court of Protection to manage the finances and property of the individual who is no longer mentally competent to manage these things themselves or who is appointed to make health and welfare decisions for a mentally incompetent person
Digital Assets	Digitally stored content or an online account owned by an individual which can include individual files such as images, photos, videos, and text files e.g. the novel written in Word and stored on the author's computer.
Disbursements	Expenses paid by your agent as part of conducting the contract you entered into with them e.g. a solicitor may pay for a local authority search as part of a property transaction and seek re-imbursement from the client

Donee	The recipient of a gift or power such as a power of attorney
Donor	The giver of a gift or power
Easements	A right to cross or otherwise use someone else's land for a specified purpose e.g. to allow water pipes to pass under your land for the benefit of other users
Equity	In simple terms it is the value of what you own in a property e.g. you might own 50% of its value and someone else might own the remainder; or your mortgage lender is owed a certain amount and the remainder is your equity in the property.

It is also means being fair and hence it is a body of law which seeks to balance the strict outcome of a law applying unfairly in some circumstances e.g. you may leave your property under your Will to whoever you like but if you promised it to someone else whilst you were alive then equity may hold you to that promise in certain circumstances. |
Estate accounts	The accounts prepared by personal representatives to show how the assets of a deceased person have been used and distributed
Estate Administration	The process of handling the settling of all liabilities and transferring assets to the correct persons or organisations on someone's death
Execute	Sign e.g. to execute the Will is to sign the Will correctly
Executors	The persons appointed by the Will maker to administer his or her estate on death
Expedition fee	The additional cost of asking for priority and speed of action in a matter over and above the normal processing fee

FD LPA	Financial decisions Lasting Power of Attorney
Grant of Letters of Administration	A formal document issued by the Probate Registry confirming the administrators authority to act in the administration of the specific deceased person's estate
Grant of Probate	A formal document issued by the Probate Registry confirming the executors authority to act in the administration of the specific deceased person's estate
HCD LPA	Health and Care Decisions Lasting Power of Attorney
HMRC	Her Majesty's Revenue and Customs
IHT	Inheritance Tax
Inheritance (Provision for Family & Dependants) Act	An act enabling certain persons to challenge the reasonableness of the financial provision made for them under the deceased's Will or the Intestacy Rules
Intestate	A person dies intestate if they have made no valid Will
Intestacy Rules	The statutory rules which apply to determine who benefits and to what extent when the deceased dies without a valid Will
Issue	Child or grandchild is one particular generation of a family. Issue is the whole line which flows down from an individual until it ends by dying out
Joint tenants	Co-owners of property who together own the whole property and its proceeds of sale such that on the death of one the remaining co-owner(s) inherit their interest automatically e.g. a husband and wife might own their family home as joint tenants if the wife dies first the husband automatically becomes the sole owner of the whole property

Joint/Joint & Severally	In the context of powers of attorney a person granting the power can choose to appoint two or more attorneys jointly or jointly and severally. The former means the attorneys can only act together in unison so that if one disagrees nothing can be done. If one joint attorney dies or is otherwise unable to act the power of the other attorney ends. By contrast, if the attorneys are appointed jointly and severally each attorney can act independently of the other so that the power will not come to an end on the death say of one of the attorneys. The surviving attorney(s) carry on without the deceased one.
Jurisdictions	A legal geographic area which submits the citizens of that area to the same laws e.g. for most taxes the UK will be the jurisdiction but for other laws the citizens of England often are subject to different laws to the citizens of Scotland
Legacy	An entitlement or benefit under a Will or Intestacy Rules (statutory legacy)
Legal Services Board	The overarching regulator of the regulatory bodies supervising those providing regulated legal services in England & Wales
Liquid assets	Cash or assets which are easily converted into cash e.g. quoted shares
LPA	Lasting Power of Attorney
MCA	Mental Capacity Act 2005
Money Laundering	The act of placing or hiding the proceeds of crime into the financial system so achieving untainted money e.g. evading a tax, such as income tax, by not putting cash tips as a hairdresser on your tax return. Then putting the tips into your bank account and using the balance in the account as normal

Nil rate band	The amount of capital value which a person may transfer on death or during lifetime without a charge to inheritance tax as the tax rate on the band is 0%
Oath	A sworn statement of truth as to the contents of the statement
Office of the Public Guardian	The administrative branch of the Court of Protection carrying out the work of the Public Guardian
Open market value	The value which an asset would achieve if placed on the market for sale on the assumption that it could be freely sold by a willing seller to a willing buyer able to proceed
OPG	Office of the Public Guardian
Panel deputy	A Deputy appointed by the Court of Protection from a list of vetted professionals usually a solicitor
Paralegal	A person who may be trained in certain legal matters but who is not qualified as a lawyer
Powers of Attorney	A document authorising a person or persons of the donor's choice to manage their affairs, usually financial and property affairs
Practitioner	In the context of this book a lawyer
Pre-Nuptial Agreement	An agreement entered into between two people before they marry setting out the financial division of assets on separation and divorce often used where the ownership of assets by each party prior to marriage is significantly different
Pro bono	Work done without charge or at a reduced rate for the good of the community
Probate Registry	The service of the Ministry of Justice which confirms the validity of Wills and issues Grants of representation in the estates of deceased persons to those it authorises to act in the administration

Receivers	The old name for Deputies in the Court of Protection
Regulated Professional	Those members of the legal services industry who are regulated by a regulator e.g. the Solicitors Regulation Authority in the conduct of reserved and other legal services
Reserved activity	Those legal activities which the law specifies must be undertaken only by regulated practitioners for the protection of the service user
Residence Nil rate band	An additional amount of value free of Inheritance Tax on death where the deceased leaves a qualifying residential interest to lineal descendants
Residual beneficiary	A beneficiary is someone who benefits from a gift under a Will or under the Intestacy Rules or under a trust. The residue is what is left after all other gifts, expenses and taxes have been paid; hence the residual beneficiary is the person or organisation which benefits from the net estate after all other expenses and gifts have been disbursed
Residue	The net estate available for distribution after all taxes, expenses and legacies have been met
Revoke	Take back – if a Will or power of attorney is revoked it is effectively cancelled
Settlement	The assets given to trustees of a trust which is subject to inheritance tax for the trustees to manage
Severance	The act of changing from joint tenants ownership to tenants in common ownership in the context of co-owning a property
Stamp Duty Land Tax	A tax payable on transactions in land on certain conditions

Successive	One after the other – in the context of trusts, successive life interests would mean one life interest will come to an end on the death of the person enjoying it and another one would start
Tenants in common	Where co-owners of land choose to own a specific share in the value of the property which can be identified and passed to someone else rather than their co-owner as part of their estate on death e.g. cohabitants Jack and Jill co-own their house as tenants in common as to Jack 75% and Jill 25% so each of them can leave their share to whoever they like
Threshold	Point at which something changes e.g. the nil rate band threshold is £325,000 above which inheritance tax is payable at potentially 40%
Title	Your title is your status such as Mr, Mrs, Ms. In property terms it is also the established chain of ownership to the property so you would have full legal title to your property
Trust Corporation	A special type of company which is authorised to manage trusts
Trusts	An obligation placed on trustees by an individual (known as a settlor) to manage assets transferred under their control for the benefit of the objects of the settlor's generosity (who are known as beneficiaries)
Unregulated provider	A person or organisation providing legal services who is not subject to the regulatory requirements of a sector regulator i.e. is potentially uninsured and untrained for the work

Chapter 1: What you need to know to get the best out of the lawyers who help you move house

1.1 The conveyancing process

The process of buying or selling a property or buildings in England and Wales is called conveyancing – i.e. you convey or transfer a property from one owner to another. It is a regulated service so only those permitted under the Legal Services Act 2007 can conduct this work, which means it is limited to solicitors, legal executives or licensed conveyancers (see Chapter 14).

The current process does not work satisfactorily. It is dependent on both a seller and a buyer being ready to agree a move and having all the people in their chain ready, willing and able to proceed. This means that neither you nor your chosen lawyer has control over the process. Chains break down; people do not always tell the truth about having their mortgage offer; problems with the legal title or planning often crop up when the process is well underway. Transactions do fall through when you may well have spent money on searches and surveys which are then wasted as well as expended time and energy on the matter. For a useful summary of what is involved see: https://www.gov.uk/buy-sell-your-home.

At the moment the sale process works as follows:

Seller
- Instructs an estate agent to sell property
- Instructs a conveyancing lawyer to act on their behalf
- Obtains an Energy Performance Certificate

Legal
- Lawyer obtains documents of title and produces sale documents to buyer's conveyancer
- When buyer is satisfied and ready contracts are exchanged - fixes price; terms of sale and date for moving house when proceeds of sale are paid over
- If there is a mortgage on the property the lawyer will need to use the money received to first of all discharge the mortgage before paying any balance as directed by the seller

Practical
- Need to organise final readings of utility services, any changes of insurance and removal firm
- Pack and clean

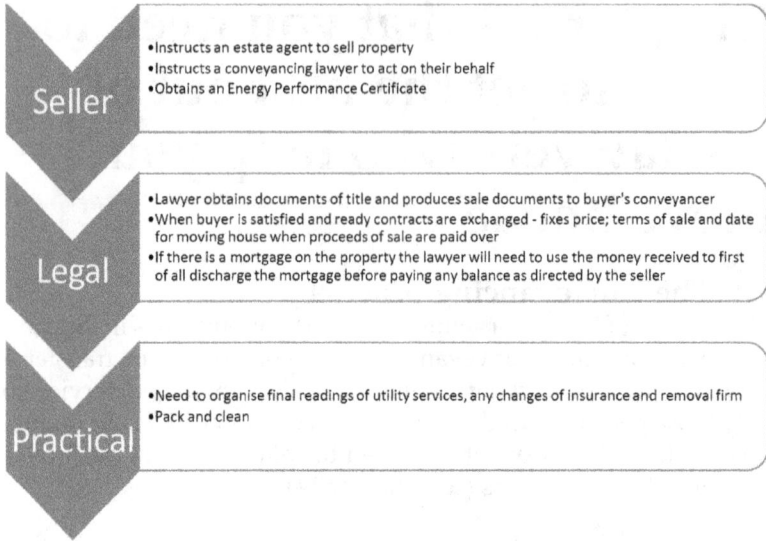

Most people who have moved to a new house will tell you that it is one of the most stressful things they have done. Obviously, how a particular person copes with moving will depend on all sorts of personal issues, such as whether this is a forced move due to a job relocation, divorce or mortgage re-possession or whether it is a positive choice to that little cottage in the country you have always wanted. If you are managing the move on your own and you have all the time in the world then it probably will not be as stressful as moving a family whilst both parents are working!

The buying process works like this:

Buyer makes offer & once acepted proceeds	Buyer applies for mortgage
Buyer appoints a conveyancer to act who must check sale documents	As part of satisfying the mortgage lender on the title, Local Authority searches and other enquiries are raised
Buyer has to be satisfied that all questions have been answered satisfactorily before exchanging contracts and taking on insurance risk	A mortgage lender will insist on a valuation survey and a buyer may need a full structural survey to avoid any nasty surprises
Buyer must have all funds necessary to cover not just the purchase price but Stamp Duty Land Tax and legal fees and expenses before committing to the purchase	Conveyancer has to report on the legal title to the mortgage lender and ensure the company is satisfied before exchange of contracts
Buyer organises move and taking over of the utility services for the day of completion	On purchase the mortgage funds must be secured by the registration of the mortgage on the legal title by the conveyancer
Conveyancer organises the registration of the legal title in the buyer's name and pays any Stamp Duty LandTax which may be due	

In many, if not most cases a person is both selling a house and buying another one at the same time. This is particularly stressful if the two transactions must be synchronised so that they share the same date and time of exchange of contracts and the same day for moving.

Some people, if they can afford it, decide to sell their house and move into rented accommodation for a short period to break up the need to synchronise the two transactions. Those that can do this also improve their chances of getting a good deal on the property they wish to purchase as they will have no chain below them to synchronise too and may even be a cash buyer, with no need for a mortgage, if they are trading down market and have sufficient net proceeds of sale from the property they sold.

It can take 13 – 15 weeks on average to complete a transaction in England and Wales, so there is plenty of time for changes of heart or problems to become evident. Strangely, this is much longer than it used to take 40 years ago. The system is not fit for purpose.

The main causes of the delay in England and Wales are:

- The identification process legally required of the people involved in the transaction
- Checking that the source of funds is not the result of money laundering
- Obtaining Local Searches – these are searches made of the Local Authority for the district in which the property is located, which are essential to check planning and other important matters affecting the property, such as roads. These can take anything from 10 – 60 days to be obtained. There are other searches too such as for water and drainage
- Obtaining mortgage finance – this often takes time to arrange and when the offer is produced in writing it may be subject to conditions which need investigation or which prevent the buyer from proceeding
- Dealing with enquiries generated on the receipt of information such as the Local Authority Search or from a review of the legal title or survey; some of which may come 'at the last minute' and result in a drop in the offered price, which could break the deal

Until contracts are exchanged the deal is not final – either party can withdraw without penalty. This adds to the stress since both parties may have invested time and resources to get to this point only to find their transaction does not proceed.

Once contracts are exchanged the parties are committed to the transaction; the price is fixed and there are serious ramifications if either party fails to complete. For example, if the buyer pulls out because the mortgage offer is withdrawn then the buyer forfeits any deposit paid on exchange. This is usually a significant sum, such as 10% of the purchase price.

1.2 What can you do to improve your experience?

A. Be realistic & flexible – it is unlikely that as only one party in the process you will be able to change things – for example, it is rarely, if ever, possible to persuade a mortgage lender to change their demands. Your move may not go according to plan so get started on some of the tasks you need to undertake in good time (such as clearing out the shed) so that you can bring forward a moving date, if necessary. Have a back-up plan in case the transaction goes slowly for any reason, such as finding temporary accommodation if you need to secure your sale even though you have not secured the property you wish to buy. Also, ask the seller or buyer non-legal questions, such as how the central heating works, don't use the conveyancer for things like this – it only delays matters and can cause confusion – a bit like Chinese whispers!

B. Be prepared – search and find all relevant legal documents you may have about your property from planning documents for that new extension to the FENSA certificate for the installation of new windows, to guarantees for any work done or certificates of insurance which were required because of a gap in the legal title. From a buyer's perspective, start from the outset and keep all such important documents in a folder or box and add to them during your period of ownership. It will definitely help when you come to sell. Better still, scan them all into your computer too so you can access them easily and forward them to your chosen conveyancer when the time comes. Also, if required, arrange your mortgage so you have an 'in principal' offer from your chosen lender.

C. Appoint a reliable conveyancing lawyer – the sooner you do this the better so that the legal preparatory work can be undertaken before you get a buyer or find your dream home. This will be a solicitors' firm or legal executive's practice or a licensed conveyancers' firm. Sometimes these firms are organised as a company and the work is undertaken by paralegals under the supervision of a regulated person. As indicated in Chapter 13, your choice will depend on whether you need more or less support throughout the transaction and the price you are prepared to pay. Hiring a reputable conveyancer who will do their best to protect your interests is vital. Always seek a quote and obtain more than one from different regulated firms before making your decision. See Chapter 13 for ways to find a lawyer.

D. Flat owners and leaseholders – should obtain from the landlord's managing agents receipts to show the ground rent and service charges have been paid. You will also need to acquire copies of the maintenance records for the common parts and any management company reports on e.g. the maintenance plans such as repairing the roof or painting the outside of the block of flats.

E. Obtain a survey – when you are buying a property you will need a survey, especially if you require a mortgage as the mortgage lender will need a valuation to ensure they are taking no risks on lending you the money. You need to budget for the cost of the survey in addition to the conveyancer's charges. If the mortgage company does not insist on a particular surveyor then ask your conveyancer for a recommendation or seek a suitable one from the Royal Institute of Chartered Surveyors https://www. localbuildingsurveyor.co.uk/?gclid=EAIaIQobChMIwo2txe672AI VyrvtCh3X2AT7EAAYASABEgJNGvD_BwE

F. Budget – Conveyancing costs and surveyor's fees are not the only items to budget for – you will probably need a removal firm to help pack and move your belongings. To budget for this a company called 'Really Moving' has a helpful calculator on their website https://www.reallymoving.com/moving-cost-calculator. Also, remember to allow for Stamp Duty Land Tax charges on a purchase (which can be significant – https://www.gov.uk/stamp-duty-land-tax/residential-property-rates). It will be helpful to consider your cash-flow leading up to and following your move as:

- Your payment dates on a new mortgage may differ from your old one
- There may be apportioned charges to pay when you are buying a leasehold property such as a flat
- Your salary payment date may change depending on whether you are re-locating for a new job or are staying with your current employer.
- There are always hidden expenses following a move so time spent trying to identify all likely impacts on your cash-flow will be time well spent.

G. Undertake some practical preparation – allow plenty of time to decide which possessions you are taking with you and what you intend to discard or give away so you only have to pack the items you plan to keep and take to the new home. Do a few visits to the new area before the moving day so that you can work out routes to take the children to school; where the relevant shops are and the layout of the nearest town or village. It is very helpful to have a map of the area. Ask for a detailed map of the property too from the estate agents so that you can check this against what appears on the ground and alert your conveyancers to any differences. Pack a bag of essential items for the day of moving such as sufficient medication, mobile phone and charger, snacks and water. Book a cleaning service to clean up after you have left your property and for the new property before you move in. For a comprehensive checklist see https://www.reallymoving.com/help-and-advice/moving-house-checklist

1.3 Possible change ahead

It is also worth noting that the Government called for evidence about the conveyancing process in October 2017 and asked:

- How would a predominantly digital conveyancing process affect home buyers and sellers?
- What should the government do in order to drive innovation in the home buying and selling process?
- How could other parts of the home buying and selling process be improved through better use of digital technology?

Ten years after it gave up its previous attempt to modernise the conveyancing process the Government sought views this time on how to make the process of home buying and selling cheaper, faster and less stressful – https://www.gov.uk/government/uploads/system/uploads/attachment_data/file/653789/Home_buying_and_selling.pdf

The consultation paper acknowledges that whilst there has been real innovation in the property search market with buyers able to search for a property online, there has been less private sector innovation in the official search and legal conveyance stages of the home buying process. One or two firms have invested in an online conveyancing system and the Government is clearly interested in seeing e-conveyancing develop a 'digital revolution in conveyancing'.

The call for evidence says:

> "To provide a firm foundation for a digital revolution in conveyancing, the government will continue to work with HM Land Registry to explore how data on property, such as leases, restrictions, covenants and easements, can be made available

more easily. The government believes that this will improve the transparency of the purchase process and allow the private sector to create innovative ways to use this information."

More controversially, the Government has asked whether there would be an advantage in encouraging buyers and sellers to use the same conveyancer. It is hard to see how this would work without causing conflict of interest problems.

The present system places the onus on the buyer's conveyancer to ask all the relevant questions and advise the buyer on whether to buy as a result of the answers provided. This is known as the 'caveat emptor' principle, which means 'let the buyer beware'. In other words, the risk is with the buyer. If they do not ask a relevant question, such as 'why is the fence to the back garden further away from the house than is shown on the title deeds?', then the seller is not obliged to volunteer the reason for this (they may have encroached onto someone else's property and may or may not have obtained good title to it). In such a situation it would be impossible for the same conveyancer to act for both parties without being in a conflict of interest position.

In France, notaires are effectively agents of the state and simply transfer ownership of a property from the seller to the buyer and collect the property taxes. They do not necessarily provide advice to either party. For example, they are not obliged to discuss the different ways in which two or more people may buy a property and the consequences of each method; whereas in England and Wales this is essential.

Professional bodies, such as the Law Society, have responded to the call for evidence.

The response of The Law Society, the trade body for solicitors can be found at https://www.lawsociety.org.uk/Policy-campaigns/ Consultation-responses/improving-the-home-buying-and-selling-process. Among other things the Law Society says that 'solicitors and licensed conveyancers are highly regulated, and we believe that the process would be improved if estate agents were subject to some increased regulation' so that minimum standards of behaviour could be enforced across the home buying process e.g. estate agents should be obliged to tell the buyer they act for the seller and say whether they have received a referral fee from the conveyancer.

It also supports the suggestion that home buyers and sellers should be made aware of their rights and responsibilities as soon as possible in the process. The Law Society has called on the government to ensure that consumers have access to an overview of the process and the potential costs and fees involved, at the beginning of the transactions.

The outcome of this review could change the way the conveyancing process is delivered in the future.

1.4 Co-ownership

As mentioned above, in England and Wales two or more people buying a property together need to decide how they are going to share the ownership. There are many reasons why people co-own property, including:

- They are married or in a civil partnership
- They are cohabiting but not married or in a civil partnership
- Parents helping a child purchase their property
- A child helping a parent purchase a property
- Relatives inheriting a property and deciding to keep it and let it out
- Business owners sharing the property
- Buy-to-let landlords investing together to build a portfolio

Whatever the reason for the joint purchase you need to ask yourself what you would expect will be the outcome if you fall out or if one of you dies. What would you want to happen and does the other person(s) agree?

There are two different ways to co-own property:

- **As joint tenants** – which means that all co-owners together own the property. If one of the co-owners dies then the others automatically acquire the deceased's share without any court action or paperwork, simply evidence of the death i.e. their death certificate. If Joe and Sue are married and buy their home as joint tenants, when Joe dies Sue automatically owns the whole property. The deceased's share does **not** fall into their estate on death to be distributed under the Will or intestacy. This choice is common for married couples and some civil partners but would perhaps not be the choice of those married for the second time who have children from their first marriage who they wish to benefit.

- **As tenants in common** – which means that each co-owner owns a specified share in the financial value of the property known as 'the equity'. This will mean that on the death of one co-owner their specific share in the equity, say 50%, will fall into their estate on death and pass under their Will or intestacy. It will **not** automatically accrue to the surviving co-owner, even if they are the surviving spouse or civil partner. For this reason, this type of co-ownership is popular where business interests are owned or where the parties are anxious to pass the value in the property to someone other than the surviving co-owner(s); or where different contributions have been made to the purchase price.

This choice of co-ownership question is most important because if, for example, on divorce the property must be divided between the parties, the presumption is that where property is bought as joint tenants the starting point (unless there is strong evidence to the contrary) for division is an equal split e.g. 50:50.

In a contentious matter, legal advice about changing the type of ownership to preserve your interest in the property and prevent transactions taking place which affect it or its value or the amount of equity left in it (such as re-mortgaging it) will need to be taken. A solicitor or conveyancer will be able to help with this and family law specialists are familiar with this problem.

Co-ownership of property between cohabitants is a difficult subject because who wants to determine what should happen to the property if the relationship breaks down when all is happiness and joy at the outset! Sadly, in too many cases, lawyers struggle to get the purchasers to focus on the importance of setting down in writing (in a document known as a Declaration of Trust and sometimes also a Cohabitation Agreement) what is to happen in such a situation.

For example, if Anne and Damian start a cohabitation relationship and wish to buy a house together will they both be happy to have acquired 50% of the value of the equity on the breakdown of the relationship? Anne works for Apple and has a high salary, contributed all of the deposit and 75% of the mortgage repayments; whilst Damian is a freelance personal trainer who had no savings and no regular income so only contributes 25% of the mortgage repayments.

Time spent reflecting on this is time well spent as any conveyancer will expect you to make up your mind when drafting the legal documents for the purchase. Incidentally, you should ask for a quote for preparing a Declaration of Trust (and any ancillary documents) when you ask for a quote for the conveyancing transaction as this will be an extra cost.

1.5 The Law Society Conveyancing Quality Scheme (CQS)

The CQS was created in 2011 to provide a recognised quality standard for residential conveyancing practices. A firm of solicitors which has gained the CQS demonstrates a credibility which other stakeholders in the process value. This is not just a benefit for house buyers and sellers but also for regulators, lenders and insurers.

The CQS system has helped to deter fraud and continues to drive improvements in standards in the conveyancing sector.

You can see if a firm is an accredited member of the CQS by looking for this symbol on their website, letterhead or other literature:

For more information about the CQS see http://www.lawsociety. org.uk/support-services/accreditation/conveyancing-quality-scheme

1.6 Checklist
• Once you have decided to sell or buy instruct your chosen lawyer – read Chapter 13 about the different lawyers and Chapter 5 to learn more about costs

- If you are selling, find all relevant legal and other documents relevant to your property (see 1.2 above) and give them to your chosen lawyer
- If you are buying, start the mortgage application process even before you make an offer on a property to obtain an in principle green light from the lender
- If you are buying, arrange a survey
- If you are buying seriously consider how you wish to co-own the property if you are purchasing jointly with someone else (see 1.4 above). If you are unsure, seek the advice of your chosen lawyer
- Whether you are buying or selling prepare a budget and cash-flow projection for the transaction so there are no surprises
- Make practical preparations for the move – see 1.2 paragraphs A and G above

Chapter 2: What you need to know to get the best out of lawyers who help you to get divorced

When divorce or dissolution of a civil partnership rears its ugly head in your life, domestic life will change forever and undoubtedly personal feelings will be battered and bruised. This does not place you in a good position to seek help nor to be able to listen to it when it is offered. You will therefore not be pleased to hear that family law, the law which governs divorce and ancillary matters, is out of date and the financial support to seek help has been taken away for all but the most difficult situations such as care proceedings in relation to children.

In order to get divorced in England and Wales you must show that your marriage has irretrievably broken down on one of five different grounds:

- Adultery
- Unreasonable behaviour
- Desertion
- Living separately for two years with consent
- Living separately for five or more years without consent

You can find more details about these grounds here https://www.gov.uk/divorce/grounds-for-divorce

It is worthwhile considering taking a trusted friend or family member with you to any meetings with lawyers and advisers since it is often hard to take in information when you are under stress. If nothing else they can take notes for you to read later as a reminder.

Family law can be offered by both regulated and non-regulated providers (see Chapter 13) so again this area of law makes it hard to find the right sort of service for you. You may benefit from counselling services to help with the trauma of the dissolution of your relationship and certainly when it comes to trying to reach an amicable settlement between you and your ex it is a requirement of the legal system that mediation is sought.

The Family Mediation Council (FMC) is trying to get all mediators accredited. Family mediation is where an independent, trained professional helps you and your ex to work out an agreement about issues such as arrangements for your children or your finances. Find out more about this on the FMC's website https:// www.familymediationcouncil.org.uk

Some lawyers will work closely with suitable counsellors who will support you through the emotional journey. This helps on many levels – not least in keeping you sane, but also in enabling you to later focus on the legal side of things. It also helps to keep the costs of the process down and hopefully there are fewer things to fight over when you deal with the emotional side of things.

Do remember though that many couples either choose not to marry or drift into a relationship but do not get married. Family law does not treat married and unmarried people the same on the dissolution of the relationship. Whilst the state of family law is not wonderful (on the breakdown of a marriage or civil partnership), it does not provide for what should happen on the failure of a cohabitation relationship.

The division of assets between cohabitants comes down to who owns what under civil law (which is a complicated mixture of contract law i.e. on what basis you acquired assets and courts deciding on remedies which can change this through promises made between you and financial evidence) not who needs what to manage. This comes as a shock to many people.

Some firms provide useful factsheets available on their websites, to explain the divorce process and some of the ancillary matters e.g. https://www.familylawpartners.co.uk/resources

2.1 Paying for legal advice

Legal Aid is a government financed support system for those who cannot afford to pay for certain legal services themselves. As of 1st April 2013, legal aid for divorce cases in England and Wales has been withdrawn by the government and you will no longer be able to obtain legal aid funding for your divorce or family law case unless you are a victim of domestic violence. To check out whether you are eligible for legal aid look at this website https://www. gov.uk/check-legal-aid

These changes have forced most people to seek to undertake some or all of the dissolution process themselves. Hazel Mantelow of Family Law Partners (https://www.familylawpartners.co.uk/ meet-the-team/hazel-manktelow) estimates 50% of clients would seek to 'unbundle' the legal service of divorce (i.e. only pay for some parts of it to be done by a lawyer) because very few people can afford to pay for a lawyer to undertake the whole process on their behalf.

Online you can find companies which offer divorce or dissolution services of varying kinds. What is offered varies in price and also in the level of support given. Do check what will be covered by the fee – often it is only the provision of forms to get the actual divorce and no help with reaching a financial settlement.

Regulated lawyers, such as solicitors and alternative business structures do offer competitive prices for divorce or dissolution work (see Chapter 14 which explains the regulatory system and the advantages of using a regulated provider.) You can ask for a fixed fee for the divorce or dissolution and often they will offer a fixed or capped fee for helping to sort out your finances.

2.2 DIY

When emotion is raw and it is hard to focus it might not be easy to undertake the divorce or dissolution process without some help. However, if both you and your partner have decided to part, and you are sanguine about it, you can do most of the work yourselves. A useful website to take you through the process is provided by the Money Advice Service – https://www.moneyadviceservice. org.uk/en/articles/diy-do-it-yourself-divorce-or-dissolution and you can find the relevant forms to complete and supply to court at https://www.gov.uk/divorce/file-for-divorce

You should not confuse getting divorced with the whole business of parting company with your ex. Divorce is merely the act of dissolving the marriage or civil partnership and you can probably undertake this without advice. However, you will need to separate your finances and if you have any children, make proper provision for them. These issues are often much more complex than terminating your marriage or civil partnership. This is where taking legal advice from a specialist family lawyer comes in.

2.3 Financial settlement

A financial settlement can be negotiated between you and your ex with the help of separate lawyers or it can be determined by the court. It will obviously be helpful if you can reach an agreement by consent which the court can approve but in some cases the situation is too fraught to agree the terms. Instead a court has to determine a fair division of the assets and also the income.

To be able to obtain proper advice as to your financial entitlements you need to be organised. Again, many lawyers will provide you with a checklist of information to gather in order to be given helpful advice but the following are the key pieces of information you need to investigate or provide evidence of:

- The current earnings of you and your ex
- The potential earning capacity of each of you both now and in the future
- The children's financial needs as well as other factors that may affect their future wellbeing – this is of paramount importance to a court
- The length of the marriage
- The assets of each of you including pensions
- The standard of living you have enjoyed as a couple during the marriage
- The financial contribution that each of you has made to the marriage
- Other contributions that each of you has made to the marriage which are of a non- financial nature, such as caring for the children and running the house

Please be careful to provide only information you own and do not breach the law on data protection by obtaining personal information, without consent, which belongs to your ex. This is why you need specialist advice, particularly in more complex cases with business interests and significant pensions or other investments involved. Sometimes, in difficult cases you need to involve the court in finding and obtaining relevant documents which might affect the size of your settlement.

2.4 Looking after your children on divorce

According to the Royal College of Psychiatrists on divorce a child may feel:

- a sense of loss – separation from a parent can mean you lose not only your home, but your whole way of life
- different, with an unfamiliar family
- fearful about being left alone – if one parent can go, perhaps the other will do the same
- angry at one or both parents for the relationship breakdown
- worried about having caused the parental separation: guilty
- rejected and insecure
- torn between both parents.

There is a useful leaflet on the Royal College's website about these issues – http://www.rcpsych.ac.uk/healthadvice/ parentsandyoungpeople/parentscarers/divorceorseparation.aspx which should help you address them and hopefully ameliorate their impact on your children.

The government website https://www.gov.uk/looking-after-children-divorce explains that you and your ex-partner can usually avoid going to court hearings if you agree on:

- where the children will live
- when they'll spend time with each parent

You can use a solicitor if you want to make your agreement legally binding but in England the system prefers you to reach agreement personally with your ex. Obtaining a court order is something of a last resort.

Throughout the divorce process and beyond it is vital that your children have a safe and secure place to live. For some useful tips on the factors to consider in agreeing the living arrangements for your children see https://www.sheppersonssolicitors.com/child-living-arrangements.html a useful website offered by a solicitors' firm.

It will also be necessary to consider the financial arrangements for looking after your children. You can agree on child maintenance at the same time or separately from sorting out the residence and access arrangements.

Both parents have a responsibility to provide financial support to their children, regardless of whether or not they have contact with them. Child maintenance, or child support, is a regular financial payment made towards the day-to-day living costs of the children. The parent who does not live with the child will pay this to the parent with whom the child lives.

There is again some helpful information on how to calculate the amount of maintenance on https://www.sheppersonssolicitors. com/child-maintenance.html and on https://www.familylaw partners.co.uk/resources

Grandparents can also suffer from not seeing their grandchildren (and vice versa) so do consider what access arrangements can be made as grandparents do not have an automatic right to see their grandchildren. If these arrangements cannot be agreed on a voluntary basis you can try family mediation or again, as a last resort, apply to court for a Living Arrangements Order.

2.5 Pre-nuptial agreements

A pre-nuptial agreement is not just for celebrities. It is an agreement made prior to getting married setting out the division of assets on divorce or separation. They are usually considered where one party to a marriage's wealth is disproportionately larger that the other's.

Pre-nuptial agreements are not legally binding in England but many court decisions prove that a Judge will often take the contents of such an agreement into account when considering any financial settlement provided certain conditions are met:

- You and your spouse must both have had the opportunity to obtain independent legal advice about the agreement at the outset; it is not compulsory although clearly advantageous
- You both must have made a full and frank financial disclosure of your assets prior to making the agreement. No assets were hidden
- The agreement must not have been entered into less than 21 days before your marriage
- Neither you nor your spouse was under pressure or duress to sign the agreement against your will
- There has been no significant change which would make the agreement inappropriate e.g. the birth of children.

- The agreement has to be fair and realistic. If the division of assets was weighted too heavily in the favour of either you or your spouse, the court may decide it is unfair

2.6 Using a specialist family lawyer

There are a number of situations where you will need to involve a specialist family lawyer to help you cope with some or all of the process. It is likely you will need help where:

- Domestic violence has occurred
- You cannot agree with your ex over the financial arrangements
- There is a dispute about contact with your children
- You cannot agree the financial arrangements for your children or even if agreed these are not being met
- You have a pre-nuptial agreement
- International issues are involved – perhaps you married outside England and Wales or one party to your marriage now lives abroad
- You are not getting co-operation over the disclosure of relevant information

Some firms are committed to providing a collaborative approach to divorce and separation. Take for example Simon Burge of Blake Morgan (https://www.blakemorgan.co.uk/training-knowledge/ features-and-articles/family-business) who offered these thoughts:

"Our experienced Family Law team includes members who are fully trained and qualified mediators and collaborative law experts, who can offer a choice of dispute management services:

Mediation is a private, impartial, solution-focused process facilitated by an independent mediator in which parties meet to resolve issues without the need for recourse to the courts. Mediators will not provide legal advice, but they do provide information and options to help people come to resolve issues in ways which are effective for them. Mediators are trained to help people reach agreements, preserve relationships and make the best, most practical arrangements for the future.

Collaborative law is an alternative to the traditional adversarial approach to the divorce process. Collaborative law was developed by family lawyers to manage the divorce process in a more dignified manner. It involves a series of face to face meetings, assisted by their respective lawyers, with the aim of reaching an amicable consensus. Collaborative law can also address issues that may not be of a legal nature, and allows those concerns to be addressed and looked at through the use of outside experts if necessary, for example, counsellors, accountants, financial advisers, estate agents etc."

It will be clear from this that some firms of solicitors can offer a comprehensive service which can utilise skills in mediation and collaboration, as above, but also expertise in associated areas of law such as Wills, tax advice, conveyancing and company/ commercial law. These larger firms may be necessary where you have a business, farm or other special assets to consider.

Some solicitors will have Family Law Accreditation from the Law Society which covers all types of family law work, except public law Children Act work, which is covered by the Children Law Accreditation. Members will have shown that they have and will maintain the required level of competence and knowledge, as defined by the Law Society, in the area of family law. You can find out more about this accreditation at http://www.lawsociety. org.uk/support-services/accreditation/family-law which also provides a link to a list of accredited members.

Firms which have accreditation from the Law Society can display the following logo on their letterhead and other media:

Another worthwhile organisation is Resolution (see http://www. resolution.org.uk) Resolution's 6,500 members are family lawyers and other professionals committed to the constructive resolution of family disputes. Their members follow a Code of Practice that promotes a non-confrontational approach to family problems and encourages solutions that consider the needs of the whole family –

in particular the best interests of children. Accredited members of Resolution can display the following logo

2.7 Checklist
The key to a successful outcome is:

- Be sure and obtain information about the process and a specialist lawyer can help you at the start
- Decide what you can manage yourself and what the lawyer can help with
- Discuss the costs of any alternative ways of proceeding and make a choice
- A modest bill for a meeting to explain the process, costs and your options can set you on the right path. If you go astray from the start it will often be very costly to unravel what may otherwise happen
- Do your homework on your financial paperwork as per 2.3 above so that you are equipped to visit a specialist family lawyer
- Think who would be a reliable and trusted friend or family member to attend the initial meeting with you and invite them to do so

Chapter 3: What you need to know to get the best out of lawyers who help you to make a Will

3.1 Why make a Will

Making a Will is one of life's more significant decisions and yet pretty much consistently over the years 70% of us fail to make one. Why is that?

- Perhaps you expect to die as soon as it is signed
- Perhaps you are afraid of justifying your position in life and don't want to be judged
- Perhaps you lack knowledge and understanding of why it is necessary
- Perhaps you are trying to avoid the potential conflict that approaching difficult choices might induce

Whatever the reason you may not yet have made a Will it is time to focus on why you should make a Will. It is the means by which you can:

- Choose who to administer your estate following death
- Choose the persons and charities you wish to benefit from your estate rather than have legal rules imposed instead
- Protect assets and people by the use of trusts which can be designed to manage assets for the future
- Avoid the application of the Intestacy Rules

In the absence of a Will, the law in England & Wales imposes the Intestacy Rules (see 3.4 below) which determine who benefits from all your assets on death. The people who administer your estate are also determined by these rules in that those who are entitled to your estate are entitled in a hierarchical way and in that order they are entitled to administer your estate; unless they do not wish to do so or they are unable to do so.

Your nearest and dearest may not be covered by the Intestacy

Rules e.g. cohabitants, friends, charities; whilst those who might be the obvious beneficiaries may not be capable or want to administer your estate.

It is better to be proactive and choose who you want to benefit from your estate; on what terms and when and to select the right people to deal with all the paperwork when the time comes.

3.2 Who can prepare a Will for you?

First of all, it is possible to make your own Will. Caution dictates that this may not be a sensible idea as many homemade Wills end up being disputed because they are badly worded or not valid due to mis-understanding the law and practice of Will making.

Preparing a Will for a fee is an unregulated legal service – see Chapter 14 – which means that there are lots of unregulated providers offering their services, some of which operate on the internet and others offer remote support via newspaper schemes etc. The fees charged vary widely from as little as £20 to many thousands of pounds in almost any area of the country.

The reasons you should choose a regulated provider are:

* They have to be insured
* They are subject to oversight and must always put your interests first so cannot charge you for services you do not need or which they do not actually provide e.g. charging for storing the Will in safe custody when the Will is left in a file or simply sent to the High Court under a deposit system
* As part of their regulatory framework they can only employ people who are competent to do the work offered so they must be properly trained and up to date
* They cannot simply close without making arrangements for securing files and storage of important documents such as your Will
* A regulated provider will be on the regulator's records and the regulator should have some knowledge as to what has happened to that practice should it close or merge with another one
* Ultimately, any complaint about the service offered can be dealt with by the Legal Ombudsman (see Chapter 14) and/ or by a disciplinary arm of the provider's regulator. It could, therefore, result in compensation for any loss and even in the

person concerned being removed from practice

An unregulated provider does not have to be insured and will not worry about closing their business. Some are unscrupulous in bundling services together and charging for services they do not provide. The problem is your family might have no redress if the business providing the service has closed down by the time of your death and your Will cannot be found even though you paid for it to be stored. Unregulated providers are not covered by the Legal Ombudsman scheme and do not have to offer a complaint handling system.

Sadly, this is very much an area of practice which is seen as straightforward but in fact touches on many areas of expertise and often overlaps with powers of attorney; vulnerable client matters and the needs of families who are going through divorce.

3.3 What should you expect to pay?
Depending on the complexity of your personal circumstances and the nature of the assets you own you should plan to obtain an estimate of the likely cost but weigh the price offered against:

- Whether the provider is regulated
- Whether the person helping you is a member of the Society of Trust and Estate Practitioners
- Whether the firm of solicitors actively participates in the Private Client Section of the Law Society
- Whether the firm of solicitors is accredited under the Wills and Inheritance Quality Scheme (although not many firms of solicitors are accredited)
- Whether your discussions give you confidence to trust the person with your personal information

For a discussion on pricing generally, see Chapter 5.

Will drafting is often offered at a fixed price for a simple Will. As to whether your circumstances fit within what a firm might regard as 'simple' see paragraph 3.5 below where there is listed the things which affect the advice you need.

Even if your situation does not come within the fixed price offered for 'simple' Wills most firms will be willing to provide an estimate or quote for what you need.

A pair of family Wills for a married couple or civil partners which leave the whole estate to each other on the first death and then divide the joint estate between their children on the second death would represent a typical standard pair of Wills. Unless you have special assets in your estate, such as a business or foreign property; or your estate is large and merits estate planning advice, then it is likely that lawyers will offer a fixed fee.

There will be differences in price depending on whether you want a personal service or are happy with a remote telephone service so it is hard to provide an average by way of a guide. Fees can range from as low as £200 + VAT to as much as £700 + VAT (at 2018 prices) for a standard family Will. Prices for Wills where your affairs are more complex (see 3.5 below) will vary widely. Please make sure you check the fee will cover the level of service you need. Some firms will usefully provide a short free interview to establish what your needs are and then will quote you a fee which reflects those needs.

3.4 The Intestacy Rules
The current rules apply for deaths on or after 1 October 2014 in England and Wales:

3.4.1 Deceased survived by both spouse/civil partner (CP) and issue

Spouse/CP receives	Issue receives
All personal chattels	One half of any residue on the statutory trusts
£250,000 absolutely (or entire estate if less)	
One half of any residue absolutely	

3.4.2 Deceased survived by just a spouse/CP
Spouse/CP receives the whole estate

3.4.3 No spouse/CP survives
The estate is distributed in the following strict order of entitlement, but no later class benefits if a member of an earlier class exists:

1. Issue of the deceased.
2. Parents.
3. Brothers and sisters and the issue of a deceased brother or sister.
4. Half-brothers and half-sisters and the issue of any deceased half-brother or half-sister.
5. Grandparents.
6. Uncles and aunts and the issue of any deceased uncle or aunt.
7. Half-brothers and half-sisters of the deceased's parents and the issue of any deceased half-uncle or half-aunt.
8. The Crown, the Duchy of Lancaster or the Duchy of Cornwall.

For a useful website which expands on the Rules and provides some examples see https://www.citizensadvice.org.uk/family/death-and-wills/who-can-inherit-if-there-is-no-will-the-rules-of-intestacy/

Quite often where no immediate family is alive and you are looking for uncles and aunts on both the paternal and maternal sides of the deceased's family you need the services of a reputable genealogist.

Genealogists will ensure you apply the Intestacy Rules correctly and conduct the research using experienced tools. Often they also can obtain missing beneficiary insurance for you where it is not possible to be completely certain that all relevant beneficiaries have been found e.g. finding an illegitimate child who no-one was aware of can be difficult. If this is not done the persons administering the estate can be liable to pay the found beneficiary's entitlement, which may be difficult to recover if you have distributed all the estate already. This is where the insurance cover kicks in to protect those people from maladministration.

There is no regulatory body for genealogists. They range from people working alone to large businesses each with their own pricing model. It is best to speak to more than one to choose which one seems right for you. Here are some of the main ones:

• Moore Probate Research – http://mprmissingheirs.co.uk
• Title Research – https://www.titleresearch.com/our-services
• Estate Research – https://www.estateresearch.co.uk/missing-beneficiaries
• Fraser & Fraser – https://www.fraserandfraser.co.uk/

- Finders International – http://www.findersinternational. co.uk/?gclid=EAIaIQobChMIn5byvtX42AIVarHtCh0iiQS_ EAAYASAAEgI19PD_BwE

3.5 What circumstances would or would not constitute a 'simple' Will?

The following highlight some of the key issues which tend to make the exercise far from simple, even if the outcome is a simple document, the surrounding advice to come to that outcome will require skill and incur risk over and above that of preparing a 'simple' Will.

1. Do you originate from England & Wales, live there currently and intend to remain there permanently?

If the answer to any part of this question is 'No' then you need to see an experienced lawyer who understands the impact of different domicile and other connecting factors on a person's estate.

Reason – English law applies to a person who regards England or Wales as their permanent home. If England or Wales has not always been your permanent home or is likely not to remain so then you need individual advice as to which countries' laws and taxes might affect your assets on death. If more than one country's rules might affect your assets on death then special advice will be required depending on the countries concerned and the type of assets owned. In some cases, in addition to having an English Will you may need a Will under another country's laws. As the advice needed will vary in each case a standard approach is not appropriate for your needs.

2. Do you own foreign assets such as a holiday home, shares or bank accounts?

If the answer is 'Yes' then you need to see an experienced lawyer who can access information about the law in other jurisdictions.

Reason – English law mostly applies to an English domiciled person's assets all over the world except land and buildings located in a foreign country. In order to be able to transfer assets easily on death, which are located in a foreign jurisdiction it is often necessary to use local documentation. In some countries there are restrictions on who may receive some or all of a person's estate. Sometimes you need specialist help, such as Title Research https://www.titleresearch.com/our-services/, to repatriate the assets.

This means you will need individual advice as to which countries' laws and taxes might affect your assets on death. If more than one country's rules might affect some or all your assets on death then special advice will be required from potentially several countries. In some cases, in addition to having an English Will you may need a Will prepared under another country's laws.

As the advice needed will vary in each case a standard approach is not appropriate for your needs. A telephone appointment with an experienced lawyer will enable him or her to provide an estimate for dealing with your case and to make appropriate arrangements to proceed.

3.   Is the value of all your assets after deducting all your debts worth more than £1 million?

If the answer is 'Yes' then you may need to see a more experienced lawyer who can ascertain what, if any, estate planning is to form any part of the advice you need and what sort of assets make up this value.

Reason – Everyone is entitled to transfer a slice of capital value on their death without having to pay inheritance tax (IHT): i.e. the Nil Rate Band (NRB) – see Chapter 7.

When you are married or have a civil partner, transfers of assets between you are usually free from IHT. However, if all your assets transfer to your spouse or civil partner on your death you will not have used your own NRB. It is possible for this to be transferred to your surviving spouse or civil partner. At the current time (until 5 April 2021) this means that any such surviving spouse or civil partner would have up to £650,000 of value which could pass on their death without IHT being payable. Above this level IHT will be payable at 40%.

If you own your family home there is the prospect of a Residence Nil Rate Band (RNRB) in addition for each owner as long as that residential interest qualifies and is left to a lineal descendant. The RNRB started at £100,000 (for deaths in the tax year 6 April 2017 to 5 April 2018) but rises by annual increments of £25,000 to £175,000 in 2020/21. Each co-owner may benefit from this so there is the potential for another £350,000 of 'nil rate' band.

This makes a potential of £1 million of value which could be transferred to your children say, without IHT on the joint estates of both you and your spouse or civil partner. Estates worth more than £2 million are subject to a tapering of the RNRB allowances with the result that at a certain point no RNRB will be due. Thus, higher value estates will only have potentially a joint set of NRBs worth £650,000 and not £1 million.

It is therefore important with larger value estates to understand how IHT might impact on your estate and that of your spouse or civil partner. You may wish to explore ways to reduce the impact of tax.

An appointment with an appropriate level of adviser will mean an appropriate estimate for dealing with your case can be offered and arrangements made as to how to proceed.

4.   Do you own a business or an interest in a business, a farm or farmland?

If the answer is 'Yes' then you will need to see an experienced lawyer who is familiar with commerce, working with other professionals, the law relating to property and land ownership and succession to farms and the conditions for IHT relief.

Reason – As indicated above, IHT is potentially payable on death on the value of assets over a certain value. Some assets have entitlement to IHT reliefs. Business interests and farms are special assets that can benefit from up to 100% relief – see https://www.gov.uk/guidance/agricultural-relief-on-inheritance-tax. The conditions which have to be met in order for the reliefs to apply are complex. However, as the reliefs have the effect of reducing the value of the assets concerned, so that IHT is payable only on the reduced value, they are of enormous importance and can result, in some cases, in no IHT being payable on those special assets at all.

In addition, advising on the transfer of business or farm interests often needs a wider understanding of the business and any documents relevant to the type of business model used, such as a partnership or company. Without sight of these documents no sensible adviser will be able to advise you on what is possible or appropriate nor how to deal with them under your Will.

An appointment with an experienced lawyer will enable you to obtain an estimate for dealing with your case and to make appropriate arrangements to proceed. It will usually be necessary to involve your accountant, financial adviser and any land agent in a discussion at some point to obtain a full and correct picture.

5. Have you been married more than once or been party to more than one civil partnership or are you in the process of separation?

If the answer to this is 'Yes' then you need to see an experienced lawyer who can take on board issues relating to the financial settlement on divorce and parental responsibility issues.

Reason – When a person has been married or been a member of a civil partnership certain agreements will have been entered into on the dissolution of that marriage or partnership. Some of these may affect your children, if you have any, and some of these may affect your finances. It is possible that you have a continuing obligation to provide for your former spouse or partner, even on death, and for your children.

Equally, if you are still married or in a civil partnership but are separated at present then your circumstances need to be discussed and variables may need to be introduced into the Will to deal with the possibility of staying married or in a civil partnership and for the possibility that the relationship might be dissolved before death.

The advice required in each case will depend on your personal facts so an appointment with an experienced lawyer will enable you to obtain an estimate for dealing with your case and make appropriate arrangements to proceed.

6.   Do you have children from different relationships?

If the answer to this is 'Yes' then you need to see an experienced lawyer. A common misunderstanding is how the law treats different categories of children and whether this matters in a particular case.

Reason – Under the law all children are treated equally except 'step children' in some cases. If you have legitimate children (those born during marriage) and illegitimate children (those born when you were not married) they are treated the same; similarly, if you have adopted children or had children by IVF or other special means. The use of the words 'child' or 'children' may therefore include some people you may not wish to include in your Will and may exclude some people you do wish to benefit e.g. step children. This needs careful consideration as excluding from benefit those who may be financially dependent upon you can result in claims being made against your estate after death.

The Residence Nil Rate Band can apply in a wider range of circumstances (as foster children and step children are included in the list of lineal descendants). The statutory trusts, applicable under the Intestacy Rules, include 'issue' rather than children (which is a much wider term allowing the whole of a family line to be included if earlier members in the line have died) and whether this label is preferred in a particular case needs to be explored.

The advice required in each case will depend on your own personal facts which an appointment with an experienced lawyer will facilitate to obtain an estimate for dealing with the case and to make appropriate arrangements to proceed.

7.   Are you intending to leave a significant portion of your estate to people or organisations who are not part of your immediate family or who or which are not financially dependent on you?

If the answer to this is 'Yes' then you need to see an experienced lawyer who can explain the law relating to Inheritance (Provision for Family & Dependants) Act 1975 (IPFD).

Reason – Under English law, although a person is free to make any kind of Will they like in favour of anyone or almost anything they wish as long as it is legal, the IPFD provides certain applicants with the right to apply to a Court to claim they have not been properly provided for. A court will consider exercising its discretion to make an order for financial provision for them out of the deceased's estate. This will have the effect of reducing how much is available for your chosen recipients.

Whether the choices you intend to make are more likely or less likely to give rise to this outcome will depend on your own personal facts. An appointment with an experienced lawyer will enable you to obtain an estimate for dealing with your case and to make appropriate arrangements to proceed. The desire to exclude estranged children is a powerful one and occurs with surprising regularity. If this is potentially your situation you will need advice on the consequences of making such a Will and what additional steps can be taken to discourage that child from making an IPFD claim after your death.

8.   Do you intend to leave some or all of your estate to disabled, elderly or vulnerable people?

If the answer to this is 'Yes' then you need to see an experienced lawyer to discuss the different types of arrangement available for the management of the affairs of the elderly and disabled and the array of trusts available with different tax consequences. There is also the interaction with welfare benefits to consider.

Reason – Where you plan to leave some or all of your estate to a person or persons who have special needs then often what might be required is a trust. You will need to choose who to manage the trust to control the assets given to them for the benefit of the vulnerable people for whom they were intended.

Whether the choices you intend to make are more likely or less likely to give rise to the need for a trust to be used or other special advice will depend on your own personal facts. An appointment with an experienced lawyer will enable you to obtain an estimate for dealing with your case and to make appropriate arrangements to proceed.

9.   Are you living with someone but are not married to them or in a registered civil partnership with them?

If the answer to this is 'Yes' then you need to see an experienced lawyer.

Reason – Where two people are living together in the same household but are not married or in a civil partnership the taxation consequences and legal treatment of their affairs is different than if they were married or in a civil partnership. In many cases the choices which they each may wish to make may be affected by these considerations and so may not result in their Wills being similar, which is usual with many married couples and civil partners. There may be a need to consider ancillary documents such as a Declaration of Trust in relation to their ownership of a property and a Cohabitation agreement, if not already in place – see Chapter 1. There will be a need to consider carefully the tax implications and to probably use a discretionary trust in your Wills. The advice required in each case will depend on your own personal facts.

10. Do you own digital assets? E.g. online bank accounts; cloud storage of photographs etc.

If you answer 'yes' to this question or you are unsure how to answer it then you need to see an experienced lawyer.

Reason – The development of the law often trails behind innovation in other areas of life. Who could have predicted ten years ago the number of apps, devices and electronic tools we all use every day? The problem is that the law of Wills is not up to date and if you are a savvy technical entrepreneur you will need a suitably up to date lawyer to help prepare your Will to accommodate what might be called your 'digital assets'.

If you are an ordinary member of the public you may not own an IT company but you may well have some digital assets – like money invested in digital accounts only; but most of the devices you own will probably belong to someone else – your data provider for example where you have entered into a lease to use your phone and most of the applications you use to store your music, films, photographs etc. Your use of these items will only be by way of a licence and so the digital asset will not belong to you. These type of agreements will probably die with you. See – https://www.thegazette.co.uk/all-notices/content/101190 and https://www.

lawskills.co.uk/articles/2015/02/protect-your-online-data-will-writing.

If you do not wish to leave a problem behind for your family you need to list your digital assets and discuss how you are to authorise the people you wish to administer your estate to find them and access them legitimately after your death.

The above are just some of the key areas which involve knowledge of areas of law outside Will preparation in order to provide the correct advice in the drafting of the Will. The more complex your circumstances are the more likely a higher fee will be due in order to fairly balance cost and risk for both you and the Will drafter. Please bear in mind that the more complex your circumstances the greater your need for excellent advice.

3.6 How you can prepare for instructing a lawyer to make your Will

Be prepared should be your watchwords. The more you have thought about what you want to do with your estate on death and considered the value of all your assets and liabilities before you take advice, the better it will be. It will enable you to answer the 10 questions in 3.5; to consider the type of lawyer you need and to make appropriate enquiries of suitably qualified people to help you.

Most law firms who prepare Wills will provide you with a checklist or questionnaire in advance of any meeting to discuss your needs. If you wish to get ahead here is a suitable set of questions for you to research the answers to and share with your chosen adviser.

Will Making Questionnaire

YOU AND YOUR FAMILY

1. Your Details

Forenames	
Surname	
Address	
Postcode	
Telephone Nos.	
Email Address:	
Date of Birth	
Occupation	
Your domicile	
At any time a person has a place of domicile which is originally the domicile of their father at the date of birth (if your parents were married) otherwise the domicile of your mother. The domicile of origin can be replaced by a domicile of choice if you intentionally make your permanent home in a new jurisdiction and reside there.	
Your habitual residence	
Habitual residence is the place which you reside and is the centre of your economic life	
Your nationality	
Nationality is the country to which you owe allegiance and whose passport you hold	

Are you (or any member of your family) known by any other names and do you own any assets in a different name? If so, please give full details below:

Birth Name	Alias	Assets held in this name

2. Your Husband/Wife/Civil Partner/Cohabitant

Forenames	
Surname	
Date of Birth	
Occupation:	
Address: (if different to yours)	
Please specify if this is a residential or nursing home:	
Their domicile	

Their habitual residence	
Their nationality	

3. Marriage/Partnership Details

(a)	Year of Marriage/Civil Partnership		
(b)	If you are not married or in a civil partnership how long have you been living with your partner?		
(c)	Please tick this box if you are intending to marry/re-marry/become civil partners in the near future		
(d)	Has either of you been married or in a civil partnership before?	Yes	No

4. Your Children (including your children from a previous marriage, civil partnership or other relationship) – full names, dates of birth, and address if different from yours. Please specify if any of them have children

Name	
Date of Birth	
Address	
Status*	
Any children of their own?	
Name	
Date of Birth	
Address	

Status*	
Any children of their own?	
Name	
Date of Birth	
Address	
Status*	
Any children of their own?	
Name	
Date of Birth	
Address	
Status*	
Any children of their own?	

*Natural, Illegitimate, Adopted, Disabled, Stepchild.

5. Children of your Husband/Wife/Civil Partner/Cohabitant's previous marriages, civil partnerships or relationships or children you act in the role of parent to – full names, dates of birth and address if different from yours. Please specify if any of them have children.

Name	
Date of Birth	
Address	

Status*	
Any children of their own?	
Name	
Date of Birth	
Address	
Status*	
Any children of their own?	
Name	
Date of Birth	
Address	
Status*	
Any children of their own?	

*Natural, Illegitimate, Adopted, Disabled, Stepchild.

Please note:

- Illegitimate and adopted children (but not stepchildren) generally have the same rights of inheritance as other children.
- Children excluded from benefit under your Will may have a right to claim a share of your property in certain circumstances. Please ask for advice, if appropriate.

6. Existing Will
   a) Do you have a Will already?
   b) If so, where is the original version kept?

c) Please confirm you are happy for me to obtain a copy of this.
d) Do you wish to register your Will with Certainty National Will Register? (for more information see www.certainty.com

YOUR HOME & OTHER ASSETS

7. Your Home – is your home:

(a)	Owned				
	(i) in your name alone	Yes		No	
	(ii) in joint names with your husband/ wife/civil partner/cohabitant?	Yes		No	
	(iii) in the name of your husband/ wife/civil partner/cohabitant alone?	Yes		No	
	(iv) subject to a mortgage?	Yes		No	
(b)	Rented	Yes		No	
(c)	Other – eg. provided by a relative?	Yes		No	
(d)	Lived in by someone caring for you?	Yes		No	

8. If your answer was (c) or (d) please give more details.

9. Do you have a Business?

Yes		No	

If yes: – state what business does

<table>
<tr><td></td></tr>
<tr><td></td></tr>
<tr><td></td></tr>
<tr><td></td></tr>
</table>

Is it a (tick box)

Company ☐   Partnership ☐   In your sole name ☐

Please give details of any assets which are in your name either solely or jointly with others

<table>
<tr><td></td></tr>
<tr><td></td></tr>
<tr><td></td></tr>
<tr><td></td></tr>
</table>

10. Your main Assets and liabilities in your sole name

Please list your main assets and liabilities in your sole name below and give approximate values. Please specify what any liabilities are secured on if applicable:

Item	Asset or Liability	Value £

11. Joint Assets

Do you have any jointly owned assets? If yes, please give a general description, their approximate values, the name(s) of the other owner(s) and details of any liability it is subject to.

Asset	Value £	Co-owner	Subject to a liability?

Please note: Jointly owned assets generally pass to the joint owner automatically and cannot be given away by Will

12. Assets Abroad

a) Do you own any assets abroad? If yes, please give details:

Asset Type	Value	Location

b) If yes, do you have a Will in that country which deals with that asset?

Yes		No	

FUNERAL | EXECUTORS | GUARDIANS

13. Funeral

You may specify in your Will if you wish to be:

Buried ☐ Cremated ☐ No preference ☐

Please note:

- You should make these wishes known to your immediate family as well and not rely on what is in your Will
- If you wish to leave any part of your body for medical purposes tell your family and your doctor and carry a donor card

14. Executors

You must appoint executors to carry out the instructions in your Will. It is wise to have at least two and you may appoint your husband/wife/civil partner/cohabitant as one. You should name other executors to act if he/she is unable to do so.

List below up to four chosen executors:

(a)	Name	
	Date of Birth	
	Address	
	Relationship to you	
(b)	Name	
	Date of Birth	
	Address	
	Relationship to you	

(c)	Name	
	Date of Birth	
	Address	
	Relationship to you	
(d)	Name	
	Date of Birth	
	Address	
	Relationship to you	

15. Guardians

You may want to appoint one or two people to act as guardian(s) for your children under 18. The appointment will usually only apply if you and the child's other parent are both dead. The position may be different if you are a single parent. Discuss this with me at your appointment. Guardianship involves a lot of responsibility and you should ask people to agree to act before appointing them.

(a)	Name	
	Date of Birth	
	Address	
(b)	Name	
	Date of Birth	

	Address	

BENEFICIARIES

The main part of your estate is called "the residue". (This is dealt with at question 18). Before giving away the residue you may wish to make certain gifts of cash or personal belongings to individual children, grandchildren, friends or to charities. These will be known as "beneficiaries".

16. Cash Gifts

Please give the name and address of the beneficiary and the amount to be given, with the age of anyone who is under 18. If the gift is to a charity please specify the registered charity number if known.

(a)	Name	Age
	Date of Birth	
	Address	
	Amount	£
(b)	Name	Age
	Date of Birth	
	Address	
	Amount	£

(c)	Name	Age
	Date of Birth	
	Address	
	Amount	£
(d)	Name	Age
	Date of Birth	
	Address	
	Amount	£
(e)	Name	Age
	Date of Birth	
	Address	
	Amount	£

17. Gifts of Articles

Please give the names and addresses of people to whom you wish to leave specific items, and a full description of the article, to enable it to be identified. Please note that if you sell or replace one of these items, the beneficiary will get nothing – he or she will not be given the substituted item or the cash equivalent. If the intended beneficiary dies before you and you want to provide for a substitute beneficiary to receive that item, please give details of such a substitute person.

(a)	Name	
	Date of Birth	
	Address	
	Article	
(b)	Name	
	Date of Birth	
	Address	
	Article	
(c)	Name	
	Date of Birth	
	Address	
	Article	
(d)	Name	
	Date of Birth	
	Address	
	Article	

18. The Residue

This is all that you own except jointly owned property and

the gifts made in questions 16 and 17. Please state below who is to receive the residue on your death and who is to receive it if they die before you. If there are gifts to your children, I suggest a provision that if any of them dies before you leaving children of his/her own, those children (your grandchildren) will inherit their parent's share.

The following are the more common provisions made. If you wish to use one of these tick the appropriate box; if not, please go to question 19.

(a)	Everything to my husband/wife/civil partner/ cohabitant named at question 2 above, outright, but if he/she has died then to my children, named at question 4 above, equally;	
(b)	Everything to my children, named at question 4 above, equally and any other children of mine;	
	You may choose the age at which your children will receive their entitlement. Insert choice from 18, 21 or 25 years in this box:	
(c)	To my husband/wife/civil partner/cohabitant named at question 2 above, but if he/she has died before me to the person(s)/organisation(s) named in the box below. If not in equal shares, then show the share each is to take.	

19. If none of the above choices is appropriate or if none of the beneficiaries at 18 survive you e.g. in the event of a family accident.

Please set out below who is to receive the residue and, if more than one person or organisation is involved, in what shares?

49

(a)	Name	
	Date of Birth	
	Address	
		Share:
(b)	Name	
	Date of Birth	
	Address	
		Share:

Who is to benefit if the recipient at 19 above dies before you?

(a)	Name	
	Date of Birth	
	Address	
		Share:
(b)	Name	
	Date of Birth	
	Address	
		Share:

Chapter 4: What you need to know to get the best out of lawyers who help manage someone's finances

Either you, or someone you know, may at some time need their financial affairs managed by someone else. It is better by far to have made a decision as to who you would like that person to be whilst you can and have put in place the relevant power of attorney to give the necessary powers to your chosen person. In the absence of a relevant power of attorney, in most cases the law requires a responsible person to be appointed as a Deputy by, and supervised by, the Court of Protection (CoP), a court specialising in the management of the care and the estates of the mentally ill and mentally handicapped– see paragraph 4.2 below.

Sadly, with the growing increase in the elderly and frail population there has been also a growth in the financial abuse of the elderly and vulnerable. It is therefore important to take appropriate legal advice about the sort of powers of attorney that would suit your situation; the choice of attorney and the protections which can be included in your powers to protect you or your loved ones from potential financial abuse.

To be able to create any power of attorney the donor of the power, that is the person making it, must have mental capacity. It is presumed that a person has sufficient capacity unless and until there is evidence that they do not. For this reason, in some cases of slowly deteriorating capacity, such as dementia, it can be difficult to ascertain whether a person is able to make a power or not at the particular time. This is why it is helpful to involve an experienced lawyer to ensure all proper procedures are followed and if necessary an assessment of capacity arranged. This should help to ensure any power which is made is valid and actions taken under it are not unlawful.

Specialist lawyers working in this field are likely to be members of Solicitors for the Elderly - see http://www.sfe.legal or the Society of Trust and Estate Practitioners (www.step.org).

4.1 Powers of attorney

A Power of Attorney is a legal instrument created by an individual (the Donor) to grant to another individual (the Donee) authority to act on that individual's behalf. Effectively, it is a form of agency in which the attorney owes the Donor certain duties.

There are three types of power:

- Ordinary or General Power of Attorney, the rules for which are governed by the Powers of Attorney Act 1971
- Enduring Powers of Attorney (EPA), the rules for which were originally set out in the Enduring Powers of Attorney Act 1985 but from 1 October 2007 it has not been possible to make new EPAs as the Act was repealed and the terms of operation were included instead in a schedule to the Mental Capacity Act 2005 (MCA)
- Lasting Powers of Attorney (LPA), which replaced EPAs, and their governing legislation is contained in the MCA, which came into force on 1 October 2007.

A common thread applicable to these different powers, is that they must be signed as a Deed, which means the signature must be witnessed, and be created in a prescribed form. Apart from general powers of attorney, the form prescribed for both EPAs and LPAs has changed at different times so it is important to establish whether the form used at the time it was dated was the correct form or else the power may be invalid.

The different rules and formats for Powers of Attorney are a good example of how different jurisdictions approach the same tools and processes. For example, for the Scottish approach see http://www.publicguardian-scotland.gov.uk/power-of-attorney For the approach in Northern Ireland see https://www.lawsoc-ni.org/DatabaseDocs/med_6831997__enduring_powers_of_attorney_english.pdf From this you will find that there are prescribed forms for LPAs in England; only EPAs in Northern Ireland and any power of attorney in Scotland has to be individually drafted!

4.1.2 Ordinary or General Powers of Attorney

These are useful documents whereby the Donor grants to the

attorney legal authority to act on his behalf or make decisions on his behalf and in the Donor's name. An Ordinary Power of Attorney is one which is not enduring or lasting, which means it cannot operate once the donor has lost mental capacity. It is therefore a temporary expedient.

For example, you could use these powers if you are going abroad for a period of time and you appoint an attorney temporarily to manage your affairs during your absence. These powers can be drafted to incorporate a specified authority, for example, the attorney can act in a certain transaction or for a certain period of time.

It should also be noted, that there is also a General Power of Attorney form, which is incorporated within Schedule 1 of the Powers of Attorney Act 1971, which 'grants the Attorney authority to do on behalf of the Donor anything which could lawfully be done by an Attorney'.

For a helpful website from the Citizen's Advice Bureau on this topic see https://www.citizensadvice.org.uk/family/looking-after-people/managing-affairs-for-someone-else

4.1.3 Enduring Powers of Attorney (EPA)
The Enduring Powers of Attorney Act 1985 (EPA 1985) came into force to enable Donors to grant authority to attorneys to act on behalf of the Donor, in relation to matters of the Donor's property and affairs only, which would endure in the event of the subsequent mental incapacity of the Donor.

The EPA 1985 was repealed by s.66(1)(b) of the MCA, which prevents the creation of any new EPAs from 1st October 2007. However the legal effect of an EPA already made before the date of repeal is preserved and integrated into the new scheme by s.66(3) and Schedule 4 of the MCA.

The legal authority that the Donor grants to an attorney was given immediately on execution of the EPA by the Donor, unless a condition otherwise was stipulated within the EPA e.g. that it would only be activated on the Donor's loss of mental capacity. If there is no such stipulation, then the Donor and attorney can effectively work together, making decisions in relation to Donor's property and affairs.

In the event that the Donor ceases to be mentally capable, the attorney is under a duty to register the EPA at the COP. Effectively, at this point the attorney only has authority to make decisions on behalf of the Donor. However, it is worth noting that the Office of the Public Guardian (OPG) in its guidance specifies that, 'should the Donor feel they are capable of being involved in managing some aspects, it is for them and the Attorney (s) to decide how this should work'. See:

https://www.gov.uk/government/uploads/system/uploads/ attachment_data/file/287864/EPA101_Guidance_apply_ register_EPA.pdf

4.1.4 Lasting Powers of Attorney
These powers replace EPAs in England & Wales and permit attorneys to make decisions about personal care and healthcare as well as financial decisions – ss. 9 – 14 MCA.

There are two types of LPAs:

* Financial Decisions LPA (FD LPA), originally known as the Property & Financial Affairs LPA; and
* Health and Care decisions LPA (HCD LPA), originally known as the Health & Welfare LPA.

An LPA of either sort can only be created using a prescribed form. The current version of the forms was introduced for use from 1 July 2015 and can be found at www.gov.uk/lasting-power-attorney. Unlike EPAs, until an LPA is registered with the OPG it is not effective. The fee for registering a LPA is currently £82 but see https://www.gov.uk/government/news/lasting-and-enduring-power-of-attorney-fees-are-changing as in some cases of financial hardship this fee may be reduced.

Unless a contrary provision is included in the FD LPA, an attorney will have authority to make all decisions about the Donor's financial and property affairs once it is registered, regardless of whether the Donor lacks capacity or not. While they have capacity the donor can still carry out financial activities for themselves following registration, but the attorney will also have this authority unless there is a suitable restriction in the LPA.

What follows are some key points about FD LPAs. Guidance in the role of acting as an attorney can be found on the Office of the Public Guardian website:

https://www.gov.uk/government/publications/how-to-be-an-attorney/how-to-be-an-attorney-property-and-financial-decisions

a.   Methods of Appointment of Attorneys
To be eligible to be an attorney you must meet the criteria set out in section 10 MCA i.e.

i) Be an individual who is over 18 years
ii) If the power is only in relation to the Donor's property and financial affairs either be over 18 or a trust corporation (which is a special form of company like a Bank)
iii) Note – an individual who is bankrupt may not be appointed as attorney for a FD LPA

It is also worth noting that the MCA Code of Practice: https://www.gov.uk/government/publications/mental-capacity-act-code-of-practice also recommends that a 'paid care worker (such as a care home manager) should not agree to act as an attorney, apart from in unusual circumstances (for example) that they are the only close relative of the Donor'.

It is also important not to overlook the capacity of a person appointed as an attorney. The MCA 2005 and the Code of Practice do not deal specifically with this point, but the attorney must sign a statement within the LPA which specifies that he understands his duty to act based on the principles of the MCA and to have regard to the MCA Code of Practice. The MCA 2005 specifies that an attorney's appointment will be terminated on his lack of capacity and the Public Guardian must not register an LPA if there is any objection that an attorney lacks capacity.

It is imperative that the Donor understands the distinction between the different ways in which an attorney can be appointed, the legal implications and the advantages and disadvantages of appointing attorneys jointly, jointly and severally or jointly in relation to certain matters and jointly and severally in relation to others. This is a complex area and can be easily misunderstood. Seeking a specialist lawyer's help with this is usually a sensible idea.

Many applications to the CoP are needed each year to resolve problems connected to the appointment of attorneys. If the Donor has appointed his attorneys to act jointly and severally, this means that they can act either together or individually and they must all be available to act at any time. If this is the method of appointment of the attorneys within the LPA, it cannot then be contradicted by stating that the attorneys must act together for certain transactions e.g. A restriction within the LPA specified that Attorney B could only act if Attorney A could no longer act. The Court deems this to be invalid, verifying that the Donor should have appointed B as a replacement attorney not as a joint attorney.

If you run a business, you might want one attorney to manage the business and a different attorney to look after your general affairs, two LPAs are recommended; one for business affairs and the other for general affairs.

b.   Replacement Attorneys
In case an event occurs which can terminate an appointment of an original attorney e.g. their bankruptcy or incapacity, it is important to appoint a replacement attorney.

You can specify the order in which replacement attorneys can act, which original attorney the replacement attorney can replace, which original attorney the replacement attorney cannot replace or whether the replacement attorney is to be appointed when the appointment of one original attorney is terminated, or not until the appointments of all original attorneys have been terminated.

You cannot appoint a replacement attorney to replace another replacement attorney.

c.   Instructions/restrictions
You can limit the LPA so that the Donee can only deal with specific assets. Any instructions or restrictions incorporated in the prescribed form for LPAs, if deemed valid, will be binding on the attorney. Only the CoP can overturn an instruction or restriction in an LPA.

The current version of the LPA forms have an option in section 5 for donors to tick a box stating that attorneys will only be able to act when the Donor does not have capacity. If this box is ticked it will be a restriction on the attorney's power.

Without such a restriction an attorney of a FD LPA can act as soon as the LPA is registered, although he must consult with the Donor before making any decisions. There continues to be much debate as to the practicality of including such a restriction especially as loss of capacity is usually a gradual matter and the thrust of the MCA 2005 is that capacity is both issue and task specific so that on each occasion an LPA is to be used the question of whether or not the Donor has capacity would need to be decided and if he lacked capacity then the attorney would be able to act.

The fact is that imposing restrictions on a power introduces the prospect of rejection of it on registration or the need to possibly request severance (i.e. removal) of some of the provisions in it in order to make the power operate appropriately. Restrictions can also limit the practical use of the LPA, as was seen in a case before the Court of Protection, which make it very hard for the attorneys to act.

Some sensible restrictions can be helpful in reducing the risk of financial abuse, such as requiring an attorney to have accounts prepared by an accountant or to permit delegation of the management of a share portfolio to an authorised person such as a stockbroker. However, too many restrictions can make it impossible for the attorney to do an efficient and cost-effective job.

d.   Preferences/guidance from Donor

You are allowed to state your preferences as to how the attorneys will act by providing guidance to the attorney. Although the attorney must always make decisions in your 'best interests'. This allows you to provide information that you would like the attorney to consider when making decisions on your behalf.

Please note that any guidance drafted in this section of the LPA is not legally binding on the attorney and this should be reflected in the language used.

The attorneys must, of course, consider the 'best interest checklist' set out in section 4 of the MCA when making any decision and weigh this up against the guidance and then take an overall view as to what is in your 'best interests'.

Examples of guidance can be:

- your views on ethical investments
- who you wish the attorney to consult before making a decision in relation to the sale of your house; for example, your solicitors
- who is to deal with your tax return, for example your accountants
- your views on how the to deal with interest and investment income

You can list as many restrictions and guidance notes as you want but take care to ensure that the restrictions and guidance notes do not make the LPA impractical as this could cause delay or additional costs.

e.   Provisions in relation to gifts and supporting others
Section 12 of the MCA is headed "Scope of lasting powers of attorney: gifts" and states that:

(1) Where a lasting power of attorney confers authority to make decisions about the donor's (P) property and affairs, it does not authorise a donee (or, if more than one, any of them) to dispose of the donor's property by making gifts except to the extent permitted by subsection (2)
(2) The donee may make gifts-
    (a) On customary occasions to persons (including himself) who are related to or connected with the donor, or
    (b) To any charity to whom the donor made or might have been expected to make gifts, if the value of each such gift is not unreasonable having regard to all the circumstances and, in particular, the size of the donor's estate.
(3) "Customary occasion" means-
    (a) The occasion or anniversary of a birth, a marriage or the formation of a civil partnership, or
    (b) Any other occasion on which presents are customarily given within families or among friends or associates
(4) Subsection (2) is subject to any conditions or restrictions in the instrument.

Please note this piece of law because many attorneys ignore it or do not appreciate what it means. It means that attorneys may only make gifts on 'customary occasions' i.e. gifts for birthdays, weddings or Christmas, or to charity but not otherwise. If you include a provision within the LPA which authorises your attorneys to make gifts which are outside the scope of section 12, it will be an invalid provision.

If the attorney wishes to make a more extensive gift than is permitted by section 12, then an application must be made to the CoP for authorisation. Examples of invalid provisions in relation to gifts include: gifts to reduce inheritance tax liability; helping the donor's son financially as and when he requires it; and payment of school fees for grandchildren.

The CoP's approach in relation to maintenance of a family or providing for their needs is that an attorney can only provide for the needs of a family member if the Donor has a legal obligation to maintain them. Accordingly, the CoP takes the view that an attorney can provide for the needs of a husband or wife, or civil partner or minor children but no other family members. For example, making a contribution to the care of the Donor's father was not allowed and neither was providing for the Donor's adult handicapped son.

If an attorney acts outside his limited authority to make gifts, the CoP will revoke the power of attorney.

In the event that the Public Guardian finds any provision in an LPA that it believes to be invalid, it will inform the applicant that the Donor may consent to a severance application or, if preferred execute a new LPA, if the Donor still has capacity. The new LPA whilst not including the invalid provision would hopefully achieve the Donor's aims in an acceptable way. However, Donors do not usually wish to proceed down this route as there will be another registration fee to pay.

The OPG's published LPA guidance gives information on avoiding drafting errors and more detailed guidance together with numerous cases highlighting invalid provisions. It can be found at https://www.gov.uk/government/publications/make-a-lasting-power-of-attorney/lp12-make-and-register-your-lasting-power-of-attorney-a-guide-web-version

f. Acting as certificate provider

To correctly complete your LPA you need a certificate provider. This is a safeguard to ensure you are capable of making your LPA and not being pressurised against your will. The role of the certificate provider is to confirm that as far as they are aware:

• the donor understands the purpose of the LPA and the scope of the authority conferred under it
• no fraud or undue pressure has been used to induce the donor to create the LPA
• there is nothing else which would prevent the LPA from being created

The certificate provider can be either someone who has known you personally for at least two years, such as a friend or colleague or is someone with relevant professional skills, such as your doctor or solicitor.

The LPA, EPA and Public Guardian (Amendment) Regulations 2009 SI 2009/1884 provide that a 'family member' of the Donor or the attorney (or of certain others involved with a care home where the Donor lives) cannot be a certificate provider. The people who cannot act as the certificate provider are usefully listed in section 10 of the LPA prescribed form, where the certificate provider needs to sign.

There is no definition of 'family member' in the Regulations. However, the OPG have provided a non-exclusive list of who they consider to be family members. The CoP has held also in a case that a cousin was **not** a member of the Donor's family. The Court said an objective approach should be adopted in deciding whether a person is a member of the family in each case.

g. Acting as an attorney

Before appointing an attorney you should clearly inform the person(s) concerned of the significance of your LPA and the powers and responsibilities it gives the attorney. Think carefully if you are asked to be an attorney whether there is likely to be a conflict of interest between your own interests and that of the Donor. Consider, as Donor, whether your attorney is likely to need specialist skills in order to manage your affairs and whether the appointment is joint or joint and several with a lay person.

Essential reading before agreeing to act as an attorney can be found at https://www.gov.uk/government/news/opgs-new-guides-show-how-to-be-an-attorney

A professional attorney who is being paid for their services must demonstrate a higher degree of care and skill than those who are unpaid. OPG Guidance warns that "*the consequences of a failure to understand or act appropriately in the role of professional attorney can be severe for the attorney or their organisation, including regulatory investigations, claims for financial loss and criminal liability.*"

An attorney should be able to manage money; keeping it separate from their own money and be able to demonstrate, if asked by the CoP, how the Donor's money has been used in accordance with the rules laid down within the MCA.

4.2 The role of the Court of Protection (CoP)

The CoP has ancient origins. In the Middle Ages the Crown took responsibility for managing the estates of the 'mentally ill and mentally handicapped' and this is almost exactly what the modern CoP continues to do.

Following the MCA coming into force, the CoP became the new Superior Court of record with authority over all areas of decision-making where adults lack capacity. Such an adult is known as a patient (P).

The CoP is a specialist court and the MCA 2005 provides that it may make any decision on a P's behalf itself, or it may appoint a deputy to make those decisions on the P's behalf. A deputy will only be appointed if P had not previously made an EPA or LPA appointing an attorney to make those decisions.

It is usually more appropriate for the CoP to delegate the function of making everyday decisions about a P's property and affairs to a deputy, rather than expect the CoP to make every decision itself. You may see reference in older publications to receivers. Deputies effectively replaced the role of receivers following the MCA coming into force.

Before the MCA changes, the CoP could only deal with financial matters, but following the MCA, with the introduction of what is now the Health and Care Decisions LPA, the CoP also deals with health and personal welfare matters.

Before the CoP can make any decision on behalf of a person it must be satisfied that the person lacks capacity to make the specific decision/s in question. In order to do this the court applies a formal mental capacity test set out in the MCA. The CoP has no authority or jurisdiction if the person retains capacity.

If a single decision can be made the CoP prefers to make it, rather than appoint a deputy to make that decision.

The CoP is based in London with four permanent district judges and the Senior Judge who exclusively hears CoP matters. High Court and other nominated judges outside London are entitled to hear CoP matters, but would also hear matters from other areas of law too. There are regional centres currently based in Birmingham, Bristol, Cardiff, Manchester, Newcastle and Preston. When it is more convenient for the parties who need to attend court from outside London, they will be allocated to a convenient regional centre.

The CoP's hearings are normally in private, but from Autumn 2015 there has been a pilot scheme to allow greater media and public access. Cases may now be reported, but if they are, it is usual for the parties involved to be anonymised and only their initials given.

As stated on the CoP's website https://www.gov.uk/courts-tribunals/court-of-protection the CoP is responsible for:

- deciding whether someone has the mental capacity to make a particular decision for themselves
- appointing deputies to make ongoing decisions for people who lack mental capacity
- giving people permission to make one-off decisions on behalf of someone else who lacks mental capacity
- handling urgent or emergency applications where a decision must be made on behalf of someone else without delay
- making decisions about a lasting power of attorney or enduring power of attorney and considering any objections to their registration
- considering applications to make statutory wills or gifts

- making decisions about when someone can be deprived of their liberty (i.e. prevented from enjoying personal freedom) under the MCA

Although not mentioned on their website, the CoP's responsibilities also include:

- making decisions, declarations or orders on financial or welfare matters affecting people who lack capacity
- making declarations as to whether an advance decision to refuse medical treatment exists, is valid and applicable to the treatment
- removing deputies or attorneys who fail to carry out their duties

When making decisions for P the CoP is required to consider whether the desired purpose can be achieved in a way that is less restrictive of P's rights and freedom of action. The court will therefore look at whether P would manage if they had help or for example, if they could manage minor day to day expenses if someone else managed more complex transactions for them.

Sections 16 & 17 of the MCA give details of the wide ranging powers the CoP has in relation to P's **personal welfare**:

- deciding where P is to live;
- deciding what contact, if any, P is to have with any specified persons;
- making an order prohibiting a named person from having contact with P;
- giving or refusing consent to the carrying out or continuation of a treatment by a person providing health care for P;
- giving a direction that a person responsible for P's healthcare allows a different person to take over that responsibility.

Section 18 of the MCA gives details of the wide ranging powers the CoP has from section 16 in relation to P's **property and affairs**:

- the control and management of P's property;
- the sale, exchange, charging, gift or other disposition of P's property;
- the acquisition of property in P's name or on P's behalf;

- the carrying on, on P's behalf, of any profession, trade or business;
- the taking of a decision which will have the effect of dissolving a partnership of which P is a member;
- the carrying out of any contract entered into by P;
- the discharge of P's debts and of any of P's obligations, whether legally enforceable or not;
- the settlement of any of P's property, whether for P's benefit or for the benefit of others;
- the execution for P of a Will;
- the exercise of any power (including a power to consent) vested in P whether beneficially or as trustee or otherwise;
- the conduct of legal proceedings in P's name or on P's behalf.

As you can see, the CoP has power to carry out almost any decision it decides is in the best interests of P.

4.3 Office of the Public Guardian (OPG)

The OPG is not part of the CoP, but is very much linked to it. The functions given to the OPG by the MCA are to:

- maintain the registers of LPAs and court appointed deputies
- supervise the role of court appointed deputies
- direct visits by a COP Visitor
- receive reports from attorneys and deputies
- report to the CoP on any matters required by the CoP
- deal with representations and complaints about the conduct of attorneys and deputies
  See https://www.gov.uk/government/organisations/office-of-the-public-guardian.

4.4 Court of Protection Visitors

CoP visitors provide independent advice to the CoP and the OPG on how an attorney or deputy is, or should be, carrying out their duties and responsibilities. Visitors may be 'general' or 'special'. If they are special visitors they will be registered medical practitioners with relevant expertise.

On receiving a complaint about the conduct of an attorney or deputy either the CoP or OPG will send a Visitor to interview the person who lacks capacity as well as the attorney or deputy. The visitor will report back and could be asked to give evidence in any subsequent court case.

4.5 Deputies

4.5.1 When will they be appointed?

A deputy for financial matters cannot be appointed if P made a valid EPA or FD LPA before they lost capacity. In that case, the attorney would act. Similarly, if P made a valid Health and Care Decisions LPA before they lost capacity, a welfare deputy cannot be appointed and the attorney would act. If the CoP finds that an attorney is acting outside their authority or not in the best interests of P it can revoke the attorney's appointment and appoint a deputy in their place.

The CoP will usually appoint a deputy to act on P's behalf where there is a need not just for a one-off decision, but for ongoing management of P's financial affairs. This is far more practical than expecting the court to carry out such daily tasks and decisions. It is unlikely that a financial deputy will be appointed if P's only income is from state benefits or state pension as there is a simple procedure for an appointee to apply to the Secretary of State for Work and Pensions for receipt of such payments – see https://www.gov.uk/become-appointee-for-someone-claiming-benefits. Where P has income from other sources and large capital assets (such as a valuable house or investments), the need for the appointment of a deputy is more obvious.

If the CoP needs to be fully appraised of P's financial affairs, it may appoint an interim deputy to act while the information is being gathered.

4.5.2 Who will be appointed?

Deputies can be a family member or friend but note family and friends cannot be paid for carrying out their duties, but can claim their expenses.

Where there is no family member or friend willing or suitable to act as the deputy, the CoP will consider a panel deputy. Panel deputies are solicitors from a list kept by the OPG see – https://www.gov.uk/guidance/panel-deputies-list-of-court-approved-professionals. A panel deputy will have to have satisfied the OPG that they are suitably experienced. Panel deputies are paid at 'professional' rates for the work they carry out and these costs come from P's funds.

Local authorities may also act as deputies, but as they are paid at a lower rate than a panel deputy, they are usually only willing to act if P is in residential care arranged through the local authority.

Careful consideration is given to who should be appointed as the deputy, bearing in mind their onerous responsibilities (see below). It must be someone willing to carry out those duties, but the appointment can be joint, joint and several or successive i.e. one after the other.

If the application for a deputy is unlikely to be disputed and the need for one is obvious, the order appointing the deputy is usually made without a hearing. If there is a dispute, the CoP will hold a hearing to decide on who should be appointed as the deputy.

A fee of £400 is payable on an application to be a deputy and the prescribed forms which must be completed are available at https://www.gov.uk/become-deputy/apply-deputy.

4.5.3 Security bond
On their appointment, a deputy (other than a local authority deputy), will be required to put in place a security bond with the OPG. This security bond protects P from any loss caused by the negligence or fault of the deputy. The amount varies depending on the value of P's resources. First, regard is had to the amount of funds that are in the deputy's control and might be lost on a worst case scenario. Then regard is had to the premium payable to acquire that level of security and the court sets the amount of the bond. The premium for the bond is payable from P's funds.

4.5.4 Extent of authority and responsibilities
When the deputy is appointed, the CoP will set out the extent of the deputy's authority in the appointment order. The deputy can make decisions within the scope of their authority if they are in P's best interests and only when P is unable to make the decision for himself. A deputy must bear in mind that P may be able to make simple decisions for himself still and only need the deputy to decide on more complex financial matters.

If the deputy believes it is in P's best interests to make a decision which he is not authorised to make, he must apply to the CoP either for the court to make that decision or if appropriate, extend his powers to make it.

A deputy needs to be careful if P's capacity fluctuates. In such a case, the deputy would have to consider each time if P can make the decision for himself (with help if necessary) and if P could make the decision himself at a more lucid moment. In that case and if the matter was not urgent, the deputy would need to wait for the more lucid moment, rather than make the decision on P's behalf.

Whether capacity fluctuates or not P might be able to make some decisions for him or herself if given the necessary help, in which case the deputy should not make the decision on his or her behalf.

As for attorneys, a deputy must apply the section 1 MCA principles and have regard to the Code of Practice. The deputy must always make decisions in P's best interests and take reasonable care not to cause financial loss.

By way of guidance for deputies the OPG states on its website https://www.gov.uk/government/organisations/office-of-the-public-guardian that when making a decision deputies must:

• make sure it's in P's best interests
• consider what P has done in the past
• apply a high standard of care – this might mean involving other people, e.g. getting advice from relatives and professionals like doctors
• do everything they can to help P understand the decision, e.g. explain what's going to happen with the help of pictures or sign language

The OPG also sets out that deputies must not:

• restrain P, unless it's to stop them coming to harm
• stop life-sustaining medical treatment
• take advantage of P's situation, e.g. abuse them or profit from a decision they've taken on their behalf

- make a Will for the person, or change their existing Will
- make gifts unless the court order says they can
- hold any money or property in their own name on P's behalf

Property and affairs deputies must keep their own money and property separate from P's and keep records of P's finances that they are managing. Keeping property separate is clearly impossible where P and the deputy jointly own a property. Here the court takes a more pragmatic view as many deputies, especially if they are a spouse, are likely to have a degree of interest in P's assets. However, if the deputy wanted to undertake a course of action which would give rise to a conflict, such as buying out P's share of a property, the approval of the court should be obtained before proceeding.

A suitably visible warning on the OPG's website is that a deputy who mistreats or neglects P on purpose can be fined or sent to prison for up to five years (or both).

As can be seen not all of the powers that the CoP has can be delegated to a deputy. Only the court can make a Will for P or authorise substantial gifts in excess of those permitted in the order to be made from his or her funds. The order usually permits the deputy to make limited gifts or gifts under a set threshold.

Gifts over the threshold or outside the limited statutory provision for gifts will need to be approved by the court rather than made by the deputy without court approval. Unhelpfully for deputies, there is no set threshold as it depends on P's resources. In **Re GM [2013] COPLR 290** the threshold was set by the court at gifts over the Inheritance Tax annual exemption of £3,000 plus small gifts of a maximum of £250 to ten people. By way of contrast, in **Re Joan Treadwell (decd) [2013] EWHC 2409** where P's resources were more modest, the threshold was set at £1,000 per year.

If a deputy wants to make any other gifts, such as for Inheritance Tax planning, they will need to make an application to the CoP for authority before they make the gift.

The OPG has produced a practice note on gifts (last updated May 2016) which is available at https://www.gov.uk/government/publications/public-guardian-practice-note-gifts

4.5.5 Supervision of deputies

The OPG has an ongoing duty to supervise deputies and the nature of that supervision depends on the value and complexity of P's estate. Most deputies are assessed at the general supervision level, but there is also the minimal supervision level.

An annual supervision charge is payable and is currently £320 for general supervision and £35 for minimal supervision subject to entitlement for exemption or remission https://www.gov. uk/government/uploads/system/uploads/attachment_data/ file/601084/OPG120-Deputy-fees.pdf. Minimal supervision applies in the case of a property and affairs deputy managing less than £21,000, so in most cases the general supervision fee will be payable.

The OPG may visit a deputy to check that they are carrying out their responsibilities correctly or in the case of a complaint.

4.5.6 Report and accounts

If a deputy is under the general supervision level they will have to send an annual report to the OPG explaining the decisions they've made. This report must include the reasons for the decisions and why they were in P's best interests, who else the deputy spoke to and that what they said was in P's best interests and how the deputy resolved any differences between the deputy and anyone else.

Accounts must be sent with the annual report evidencing how the deputy has managed P's finances or property. If a deputy does not send this report annually, the OPG may increase the level of supervision or ask the CoP to remove them and appoint a replacement deputy.

4.5.7 Ceasing to be a deputy

If P dies, the deputy's appointment comes to an end and the OPG should be notified. However, the security bond remains in force for seven years after P's death unless a court order is made cancelling it.

If P regains mental capacity the deputy should apply to the CoP on form COP9 for their discharge. If the deputy no longer wishes to be a deputy form COP1 should be completed. The deputyship will only cease when the CoP makes the relevant order and not before that point, except in the case of P's death.

Similar to the position with powers of attorney, if the CoP is satisfied that the deputy has acted, or intends to act, in a way which is contrary to his authority or is not in P's best interests, the court will revoke the appointment.

4.6 Checklist

- Take a look at the OPG website and decide whether to prepare the LPA yourself or ask a lawyer to do it for you.
- Because it is such an important document and you probably need advice about whether to appoint attorneys jointly or jointly & severally and advice on any restrictions or preferences it is recommended that you ask a suitable solicitor to prepare it for you who is preferably a member of SFE or STEP. He or she will be able to discuss all the relevant choices on the form; ensure it is signed and witnessed correctly, in the right order by the right people.
- Do ask your proposed attorneys if they are willing to act as your attorney and point them to the explanations online about what this entails.
- Be aware that family members and friends can be tempted by your money so choose wisely and do not be afraid to impose some restrictions https://www.elderabuse.org.uk/financial.
- When you are authorising someone to manage your finances for you, at a time when you are no longer able to do so yourself, you will want to be sure you can trust that person. If they are not a family member ensure you ask a regulated professional – (see Chapter 14), such as a solicitor, so you know that they can be called to account if anything goes wrong.

Chapter 5: Is price all you should be concerned about?

5.1 The difficulty of price comparison

In this day and age checking out the price of a product or service on a comparison web site is the norm. Successive Governments have also tried to generate competitive pricing to help the consumer by bringing competitive forces into areas which in the past were government utilities like the energy sector and telecoms.

When you want to buy oil, electricity or gas you might look at the price which is offered by the market only if you are savvy or dissatisfied with your current provider. These regular bills and variations in price mean that if it was easy to switch we would all do it frequently to save money and yet although the number of households switching is increasing most of us do not bother to switch. This is partly because it involves some effort on our part and partly despite there being a market in the provision of the service it is not a large market (30 providers) and the prices are within a range such that inertia is comfortable. Ofgem, the regulator, believe we could save at least £200 by switching, particularly if we have never done it.

Also, some of these markets have statutory regulators who can levy fines and encourage changes so this acts as an encouragement for all the players in the market to be competitive. In 2014 Ofgem referred the energy market to the Competition and Markets Authority for a full inquiry after lots of customers and consumer groups accused the energy providers of overcharging customers.

In the legal services sector the Competition and Markets Authority has also been hard at work. In its detailed report of December 2016 (https://assets.publishing.service.gov.uk/media/5887374d40f0b6593700001a/legal-services-market-study-final-report.pdf) it said that:

> "Overall, we have found that the legal services sector is not working well for individual consumers and small businesses. These consumers generally lack the experience and information they need to find their way around the legal services sector and

to engage confidently with providers. Consumers find it hard to make informed choices because there is very little transparency about price, service and quality – for example, research conducted by the Legal Services Board (LSB) found that only 17% of legal services providers publish their prices online. This lack of transparency weakens competition between providers and means that some consumers do not obtain legal advice when they would benefit from it...... We are recommending that the regulators develop new minimum standards for disclosures of price, service, redress and regulatory status, and require providers to adhere to them."

In 2017, the Legal Services Consumer Panel found that just over one in four potential clients compared legal service providers online.

5.2 Pricing models

Price is not the only factor in choosing a service but always insist your legal provider makes it clear and in writing what charges are to be made for what services and whether the price includes or excludes charges made by others as part of the process, such as search fees levied by Local Authorities which are an essential part of buying a property; or, the Probate Registry's fee for issuing a Grant of Representation when dealing with the administration of a deceased person's estate.

Of course, any price quoted would need to state whether it was inclusive or exclusive of VAT and if it is exclusive of VAT then the provider should specify the total cost including VAT, as well, so that those not familiar with this tax can see the total amount they have to budget for.

In a way price is the easy item to compare but even here the consumer needs to understand there are different types of price before any comparison on price can be made. For example, the following table illustrates some common forms of pricing in the legal sector.

	Type	Explanation
1	Fixed fee	A fixed price is quoted for the legal services, plus any extras and VAT e.g. £300 + VAT and Disbursements for acting in the sale of your property.
2.	Hourly rate	A price per hour is quoted and although no set number of hours is quoted an estimate might be given e.g. £200 per hour + VAT and an estimate of 10 hours would mean potentially £2,000 + VAT for the legal service but this is not fixed and could be more or less depending on the number of actual hours it takes. Published hourly rates may include a number of different rates depending on which sort of lawyer is undertaking different parts of the process e.g. a partner in a law firm's rate might be £250 per hour; a solicitor's hourly rate might be £200; a legal executive's hourly rate might be £150 and a paralegal's hourly rate might be £90.
3.	Blended rate	A price per hour which takes into account a number of different rates depending on status but is offered as an average. E.g. the average hourly rate in 2 above might be £172.50 per hour – a blend of all the rates. So everything would be charged at this rate regardless of which member of staff was undertaking a particular task.
4.	Percentage	The fee would be quoted as representing a percentage of the value of the assets involved e.g. 1.5% of the sale price of a property or 1% of the value of someone's company or a deceased person's estate. Percentage prices are fixed with VAT on top.

5.	Added Value or exceptional risk	An expedition fee or particular complexity which relates to your matter as opposed to the usual fee the firm would charge for similar cases. A bit like Vision Express's model of charging more for speedy service. So the standard fee for selling the property might be £500 + VAT and disbursements but because it is to be sold at auction in two weeks' time there is an expedition fee to get everything ready in a short period of time and additional insurance for lack of local authority search so it might be £1,000 + VAT and disbursements.

From this you will see that it is difficult to compare the fixed fee quoted by one firm with an hourly rate of another or the percentage charge of another. For example, if a deceased person's estate was roughly valued at £750,000 one firm might quote a fixed fee of £10,000 + VAT and disbursements; another might quote hourly rates of £200 with an estimate of 45 hours + VAT and disbursements (i.e. £9,000) and another might quote hourly rates of £150 with an estimate of 100 hours + VAT (i.e. £15,000); another firm may quote 1.5% of the value of the estate (in this example that would be £11,250. On these prices the firm quoting £200 per hour + VAT would actually be the cheapest although their estimate may prove to be unreliable. In other words, sometimes fixing the fee can be more expensive but it buys you security in knowing there will be no nasty shocks later.

Hourly rates are a reflection of how experienced, efficient and organised the lawyer might be and how well managed the firm is since the overhead costs of running the firm will form part of the level set by the hourly rate.

A well organised firm will probably have invested in suitable IT and have effective financial management by employing an experienced accountant as its chief executive. This may be reflected in a £200 hourly rate compared to £150 hourly rate in a less well invested and organised firm, where the partners muddle through.

Also, the estimated number of hours in the firm charging the higher hourly rate may be more accurate and less than a competitor because of its investment in IT and the information it can provide the firm; the volume of similar cases it can undertake because of the IT and therefore the greater experience it has in conducting the process. The estimate may well prove to be exact and there might be no surprises.

Equally, a higher hourly rate could hide inefficiencies in a firm for example, it might pay high salaries and manage its own finances badly so it needs to charge more per hour to cover its overhead costs.

These are some of the reasons why comparison websites on price are not really all that helpful to consumers in selecting the right supplier of legal services.

5.3 Is what we are paying for only the price of the product or does it include something else?

What might differentiate the offerings may well not be the price on the table but our experience of dealing with the company when things go wrong or if we need some support or specialist help. This starts to reveal that price is not the only determinant of satisfaction with something.

A wonderful gift shop sells delightful jewellery, scarves, handbags and all sorts of products. Of course you could buy some things cheaper in a chain store or online but mostly they have unique products they have sourced from suppliers personally and their prices are reasonable. However, the reason they do so well is not just their choice of products for sale and the prices they charge but the service provided at the point of sale. You see they specialise in gift wrapping – not just a tired bit of ribbon on some tissue paper stuffed in a carrier bag but the most wonderful ribbons and bows expertly created personally for you on each package. Everyone wants to receive a parcel wrapped by Forme!

You see even in comparing the price of products there is often an additional factor of difference which makes comparison difficult. Sometimes this is intentional, as we know only too well, when products are in fact a bundle of offers e.g. telephone companies which include data, texts and calls in a bundle.

There are also examples on the High Street of businesses who use price to differentiate themselves from their competitors but again include a special factor to justify the difference e.g. Specsavers, the opticians, compete on the price of their frames and were able to sell competitively priced frames based on economies of scale by buying frames in bulk in China and operating from a Jersey base. Their main competitor is Vision Express whose name reflects that their prices are not based on saving money on frames but getting a quick service so even if they cost more than Specsavers they are offering something different – a speedy service.

5.4 Purchasing Services

When we move into purchasing services it can become complex if we are not buying something routine. A routine hip replacement purchased from a private hospital will be priced on the basis that the consultant knows precisely what is involved and knows how long it will take to do the operation, providing there are no complications. If we have not had an operation before we may not know how we will respond to the anaesthetic but unless we display some kind of allergic reaction, which turns the procedure into an emergency, it could just delay our recovery and not affect the conduct of the operation. It may well colour our desire to have another operation though.

In the legal world some processes are indeed routine like buying and selling a house in England or obtaining a Grant of Probate when someone dies but the amount of work involved can vary enormously from case to case because of personal factors such as:

- **Your behaviour** – are you likely to need constant reassurance through daily telephone calls or e-mail or are you someone who is likely to agree a reporting process and stick to it?
- **The complexity** – no-one should expect the cost of buying a typical family house on an established estate in the centre of a town where the property title is registered at HM Land Registry to be the same as dealing with the acquisition of an unregistered house on a private road with private drainage comprising a let property in the grounds, stabling, swimming pool and tennis court and some 10 acres of other land.
- **The number, value and difficulty of assets involved** e.g. in an estate, if everything is jointly owned and passes on the deceased's death by survivorship then a Grant may not be

required and only a few letters may be necessary to finalise it; whereas, if there are foreign assets; business assets, lots of investments etc., then not only will your chosen lawyer be involved but other specialists too such as an accountant to value the business, a foreign lawyer to handle the transfer of ownership of the foreign assets and wealth managers to deal with the investments. The more people involved in a transaction the longer it takes and the harder it is to control when things will be in place.

- **The extent to which you can engage with the lawyer electronically** or whether it will require a more personal service because you prefer to speak on the telephone or call into the office or you need a home visit.
- **How quickly something needs to be done** – if something is needed to be done quickly to preserve it or prevent someone else obtaining it, for example, then it is not unreasonable to be charged an 'expedition fee' as other clients' cases will need to be set aside or longer hours will need to be worked or more staff employed in your case compared to the normal transaction of this type.
- **The novelty factor** – is this an unusual case where there might need to be sophisticated research? For example, in a 2017 case extensive research was required as to the deceased's intention in making the Will including: obtaining a statement from one of the witnesses to the Will confirming how it was signed; obtaining reports from the deceased's GP as to his mental capacity; making enquiries of numerous cancer charities to see what, if any, connections the deceased had with them; making interim and final applications for the administration of the estate; making an application to the Attorney General's office for a charity bequest to be cancelled; obtaining expert advice on the writing on the Will; arranging for a change to the terms of the Will by Deed of Variation to achieve certainty and obtaining expert evidence of the law of Montenegro.

A tin of baked beans is a tin of baked beans – you might pay more for a branded product rather than an own brand tin but frequently that is all. Your choice will come down to taste or habit, if you are not choosing simply on price. Getting divorced and making a Will are not the same. Even if you knew the price was fixed you might prefer talking to one lawyer as opposed to another; one service may include some counselling as well as legal advice, another may not limit the number of telephone calls you can make; or will provide a home visit; another may not provide any human interaction and simply provide the process.

Feelings and emotions will come into it and how you cope afterwards may well be determined by your experience. It is a much more significant purchase than a can of beans and sadly hard to know in advance how costly in both price and human-terms it will have been until it is over.

It is for these reasons that most people will ask friends, family and work colleagues for a recommendation before committing to a particular legal services provider. Whilst one person's experience is no guarantee that your own will be the same or similar, particularly if the service needed and the person acting within a firm may not be the same, nevertheless it is frequently a useful part of the decision making process to ask for the experience of others – good or bad.

The success or otherwise of most transactions will probably end up being a trade-off between the price, the quality of the service and speed. For example, the quicker something is needed or demanded the likelihood is that the price will need to be increased to deliver this service otherwise the quality of the service will be poor. Marketing does intervene – the canny consumer has to be willing to learn something about the market for the service they require; and not just respond to the advert of the one provider that 'shouts' the loudest.

5.5 Checklist

1. You can help yourself to find the most appropriate legal provider for you by reflecting on some of the following things and deciding on what is important to you:
   - Am I upset and so will benefit from dealing with a caring and empathetic person who I can meet if necessary rather than a distant call centre?
   - Do I have high ethical standards and therefore would like to use a supplier who supports the local community with pro bono work?
   - Will I need a home visit and so need to choose a local provider?
   - Is what I am proposing to do complicated or at least it

appears to be so? If yes, would I welcome a discussion first about the mix of legal services and expertise I will need before I commit?
- Am I likely to need a 24 hour/seven day a week operator with people available who can speak my language as English is not my first language but I need English legal advice?
- Have I undertaken this process many times and so will not need as much support as a person who has no familiarity with the service and would be quite happy dealing with a remote provider who was competitive on price?
- Is the work I need help with likely to last many years, such as operating my finances under a power of attorney or administering a trust? If so, what is the likely track record of the firm? Are they likely to still be providing the service and will the person appointed in the firm still be in post?
- Am I likely to worry about the technical skills and financial management of the legal service provider? If so, a regulated rather than unregulated provider might suit me best.

2. One or more of the items in 1 above may resonate with you. Once you have made these decisions then it will be a question of checking the relevant market place (local, national, online) to list all the providers who could meet your needs – you might be able to do this from talking to friends, family and contacts and looking at their respective websites. This research may enable you to shorten your list.
3. At this point, seek the prices offered by your list of firms by directly calling them and ask for their terms of business. Any regulated provider will happily give you a written estimate or quote for the fees they suggest or offer a free meeting to discuss the problem and then provide these things.
4. Reflect on all your research and check out any favoured persons credentials such as their qualifications and any special accreditations for them or their firm. These are often specified on the organisation's website or in the list of organisations regulated by a particular regulator (see Chapter 13).
5. The decider, when you have several possible choices still, will be who you found the easiest to talk to and who you would feel you could trust the best. These views are inevitably subjective but after all your objective testing a bit of human intuition entering the process is no bad thing.

Darren Leggett of Executor Solutions (http://www.executor solutions.co.uk) says that whilst a 'Check a Trade' equivalent would be useful for checking out providers of legal services it would need to be based on not just a list of people offering the service and not just on pricing but also a star rating system or equivalent to help people choose from other people's experience. He also suggested that it would help if there was some sort of average price for the cost of the service to help people question what they have been quoted on price and to enable justifiable differences in service to be highlighted, such as being insured; being regulated and having staff who are specially accredited.

As yet this type of service is not available but it is the sort of idea that the Competitions and Markets Authority would like to see develop.

Chapter 6: What you need to know to get the best out of lawyers who help you to administer someone's estate on death

The two biggest complaints lawyers receive from clients about estate administration cases undertaken for them are that it takes too long and that it costs too much. Most of this frustration is based on poor communication and understanding of the process. Some of the criticism is justified. If you understand the process then hopefully you can avoid these pitfalls and get the most out of your relationship with your probate practitioner.

Equally, if you decide to undertake some or all of the process yourself do not fall into the same trap of taking too long over the administration. People who benefit under the Will or intestacy of the deceased may become angry or complain; or, your failure to understand the process has cost the estate money which could have been avoided if undertaken properly e.g. tax penalties.

Please remember the persons responsible for administering someone's estate are:

- The executors named by the deceased in his or her Will – the persons concerned must be willing to act and mentally capable of acting or they appoint an attorney to act on their behalf under a power of attorney if they are competent to do so
- Where there are no named executors willing and able to act and no attorney then an adult residuary beneficiary named under the Will can apply to be an administrator of the Will
- Where there is no Will, the person entitled under the Intestacy Rules to obtain a Grant of Letters of Administration instead of a Grant of Probate will apply to be the administrator

It is always possible, and frequently the case, that executors or administrators may appoint a probate practitioner to act as their agent in the administration of the estate. The collective name for executors and administrators is **Personal Representatives** commonly shortened to simply PRs.

6.1 Coping with bereavement

When someone you know dies you will be in a state of bereavement. This loss will be felt more the closer you were to the deceased. Recognise that you may be too distraught to deal with practical matters, some of which might need to be undertaken urgently, such as registering the death.

To understand how you feel see https://www.nhs.uk/ Livewell/bereavement/Pages/coping-with-bereavement.aspx which identifies the following issues:

"Experts generally accept there are four stages of bereavement:

- accepting that your loss is real
- experiencing the pain of grief
- adjusting to life without the person who has died
- putting less emotional energy into grieving and putting it into something new – in other words, moving on

You'll probably go through all these stages, but you won't necessarily move smoothly from one to the next. Your grief might feel chaotic and out of control, but these feelings will eventually become less intense."

If these feelings are such that you or a loved one, such as a surviving parent, is not coping then consider bereavement counselling http://www.counselling-directory.org.uk/bereavement.html

6.2 DIY

If you are able to cope with your loss then you may be able to undertake the estate administration yourself. If you have acted as attorney for the deceased you may well have all the relevant knowledge about the property and finances of the deceased and be best placed to administer the estate.

It is possible to conduct the estate administration process yourself. It may involve a personal application for a Grant of Representation (a key document authorising the PRs who are charged with administering the estate to collect and distribute the assets, usually a Grant of Probate – where there is a Will; or a Grant of Letters of Administration, where there is no valid Will).

You need to be organised, numerate and good at dealing with paperwork and accounts. All the people benefitting under the estate must trust you – see https://www.gov.uk/wills-probate-inheritance

Small estates (those comprising cash assets or personal items like jewellery, which are worth less than £5,000) can be dealt with without obtaining a Grant. Many Banks will agree to release funds of up to £30,000 without a Grant – see http://www.lawsociety.org.uk/for-the-public/common-legal-issues/probate

Estates which are valued at less than the inheritance tax threshold of £325,000 require less administration than those which are taxable see https://www.gov.uk/inheritance-tax. However, there are still technical issues involved and if the estate includes a house or land then it will be necessary to obtain a Grant to be able to deal with the estate properly.

It is possible to undertake part of the process yourself and part of it with the help and assistance of a regulated probate practitioner – see Chapter 14. This is known as 'unbundling the service' and requires a clear understanding of what is and what is not to be undertaken by the regulated person.

The most common work an individual asks a regulated practitioner to perform is that leading to the obtaining of the Grant. However, do be aware that some legal documents might still be required to transfer legal title to property to those inheriting or purchasing a property in an estate and this would need to be undertaken by a solicitor or licensed conveyancer.

At the end of administering an estate those appointed as executors under a Will, or who have acted as administrators in the absence of a Will, need to be able to account for all the assets and how they have been spent or distributed. This means preparing a set of accounts which is clear and understandable.

You would be wise to consider instructing a regulated probate practitioner to act on behalf of the executors or administrators where there are complex matters in an estate to deal with, including:

* a business
* a farm
* a foreign property
* large debts which may make the estate insolvent
* potential disputes over who is entitled to the estate
* difficulties in interpreting the terms of a Will
* tax issues

6.3 Who can act for you?

This is an area of law where some of the process is a reserved activity and so must be undertaken by a regulated person when a fee is charged. The reserved activities are limited to preparing any probate papers for the purposes of the law of or in relation to any proceedings within England & Wales and the administration of oaths, which is the exercise of the powers conferred on a commissioner for oaths (which includes solicitors) – see Chapter 14.

The key regulated probate practitioners are:

* Solicitors – http://www.lawsociety.org.uk/for-the-public/common-legal-issues/probate
* Entities which are called 'Alternative Business Structures' and regulated by the Solicitors Regulation Authority e.g. the Co-Op https://www.co-oplegalservices.co.uk/probate-solicitors
* Some accountants and alternative business structures who have been authorised to undertake probate work by the Institute of Chartered Accountants of England and Wales https://www.icaew.com/technical/legal-and-regulatory/probate-and-alternative-business-structures or the Association of Certified Accountants http://www.accaglobal.com/uk/en.html
* Entities licensed as Probate Practitioners by the Council of Licensed Conveyancers http://www.conveyancer.org.uk/trainee-lawyer/Become-a-CLC-Lawyer/Licensed-Probate-Practitioner.aspx

Generally, it is thought that preparing probate papers means applying for a Grant. The preparatory work required to be in a position to apply for a Grant is thought not to be reserved but it is something of a grey area.

There are plenty of unregulated probate practitioners who may conduct most of the process on behalf of the executors or administrators under a power of attorney. As mentioned in Chapter 14 this means that they are not necessarily insured or trained in what they are doing. The resultant risk is that if things go wrong you may not be able to gain redress or compensation for any loss.

A regulated practitioner will need to supply you with an estimate of charges, transparency over how the charges are to be calculated and on what basis (see Chapter 5) and provide a set of terms of business setting out what the practitioner will be doing for you and what they are not doing.

Many probate practitioners base their charges on an hourly rate with an estimate or a capped number of hours or offer a fixed fee for obtaining a Grant or charge a percentage of the value of the estate e.g. 1.5%. Be sure to be clear what is being offered and how much this is likely to be.

6.4 The process for administering an estate

The process consists of four key parts:

| Taking on a new estate and conducting a risk assessment | Collecting, recording and using relevant information about assets & liabilities | Obtaining the relevant Grant of Representation | Winding up the estate |

If you instruct a regulated probate practitioner to act on your behalf this is likely to be how the process will unfold:

A. Taking on a new estate

Care will be taken when you contact the regulated probate practitioner to clarify who you are. This is because the practitioner may not know you or your relationship to the deceased. Until the identity of the deceased's PRs have been confirmed and those people have formerly instructed the probate practitioner to act for them in the estate then they are not allowed under their professional rules (on the grounds of confidentiality) to give out any information to others, no matter what their relationship with the deceased.

Once the identity of the PRs has been ascertained the probate practitioner will want to arrange an interview with the PRs. A face-to-face meeting is preferred. Information should be provided by the regulated practitioner to the PRs beforehand of what papers belonging to the deceased to bring to the meeting.

Regulated probate practitioners will have standard procedures which must be followed when taking on a new matter which includes conducting Anti-Money Laundering identification and verification of the PRs e.g. see https://www.gov.uk/guidance/money-laundering-regulations-your-responsibilities. If you are one of the PRs, be prepared to provide some kind of photographic identification, such as a passport, and a letter addressed to you at your home e.g. a bill or statement of an account. Please note you cannot use online bills or accounts as these can be tampered with.

Immediate practicalities include:

- Registering the death – which you or a family member would usually undertake – https://www.gov.uk/register-a-death and https://www.gov.uk/after-a-death. Always ask the probate practitioner how many copies of the death certificate they will need as it is cheaper to order these at the outset than have to come back later. Family members may also wish to have an official copy of the certificate. The registration process can be delayed if there is a post mortem or inquest.
- Locating the last valid Will so that the probate practitioner can check if the Will mentions the choice selected by the deceased for the disposal of their body and other terms. You could consider using the services of Certainty, a national and commercial Will registration service. Choosing one of the types of search offered by Certainty will help reassure you that your probate practitioner is administering the estate on the terms of the last valid Will. See https://www.nationalwillregister.co.uk. Please note that there is no compulsion to use a registration service such as this so there is no guarantee that the deceased's Will either will have been registered or may be found using the wider Certainty searches available. It will however demonstrate that the PRs did their best to find the last valid Will.
- Arranging the care and management of the deceased's pets
- Securing the deceased's house and complying with the

requirements of the insurers – it may be necessary to change the locks as in the absence of a surviving partner or other person living there it will be unknown who has a key and could gain access; also insurers will stipulate many conditions which you can help to meet in order to retain insurance cover on the empty property

B. Collecting, recording & using relevant information about assets & liabilities

The initial interview with the PRs starts the ball rolling. Some of the financial paperwork supplied by the PRs will enable the probate practitioner to identify & value the deceased's assets and liabilities. This step can involve a lot of work – the amount depends on the complexity of the deceased's estate. The greater the number of investments and liabilities a person has the more letters have to be written to ascertain their value at the date of death.

To undertake this process evidence of death (i.e. the death certificate) will need to be produced to Banks, Building Societies, Insurance companies, Company registrars etc. This is why it is sensible to ask for several copies of the death certificate when registering the death and not to request only one copy. Each company or organisation will have its own procedure for providing the necessary information and this can take several weeks to secure. The probate practitioner may have to chase up slower companies. A bad winter with a greater than average number of deaths can slow down some organisations in supplying the data.

Some assets, such as private company shares or property, will have to be valued. In a taxable estate this will usually have to be formally done by a suitably qualified expert. For example, in an estate where the deceased is not survived by a spouse or civil partner there may be a family home. Depending on its value it may make the estate taxable. PRs must supply HMRC with the correct 'open market value' for the property. A qualified surveyor may be required. Where there are business premises or a farm this will be inevitable.

New services are popping up all the time to help with different aspects of estate administration. For example, organising the valuation of a family home, putting it on the market and seeing it through the sale process can be undertaken by Executor Solutions – see http://www.executorsolutions.co.uk.

Liabilities also need to be documented. To be sure none are overlooked the probate practitioner may advise the PRs to advertise for any unknown liabilities or claims. This is an important process to protect the PRs but it can be costly as notices have to be placed in a local newspaper and in the London Gazette https://www.thegazette.co.uk/wills-and-probate/place-a-deceased-estates-notice.

The outcome of this exercise should be a schedule of Assets and Liabilities which will form the bedrock of the administration of the estate.

Also at or after the initial interview the probate practitioner will be able to confirm the validity of the Will and who benefits under it or if there is no valid Will who benefits on the intestacy of the deceased.

C. Obtaining the relevant Grant of Representation

There are two different procedures depending on whether or not there is Inheritance tax (IHT) to pay. Please note as at 1 February 2018 these processes are under review by HMRC.

If IHT is payable:

- It must be paid **before** the application for a Grant is made. Most High Street Banks and wealth brokers operating under a discretionary management service will be willing to send sufficient of the deceased's cash under their control directly to HMRC BUT in estates where there is insufficient cash or assets which can be cashed in easily in the deceased's name and IHT is due, loans may be required – either from the family or 3rd party lenders to meet the tax bill. Most people are unaware of this. Estates with high value capital assets and little or no cash will inevitably need loans which will ultimately be repaid once sufficient assets are sold after the Grant has been obtained.
- This means it is necessary to complete an account called the **IHT 400** and submit it to HMRC with the means to meet the tax – https://www.gov.uk/government/publications/inheritance-tax-inheritance-tax-account-iht400. This is a substantial piece of work – the form has many schedules attached to it. Whilst only those schedules which are relevant to the deceased have to be completed it is nevertheless a time-consuming task.

- A receipt for the IHT is required from HMRC to pass to the Probate Registry – sadly, in 2017 delays of 8–10 weeks were experienced for this, which was unusual. HMRC have put in place some improvements but it is still taking longer than it should. This is not the probate practitioner's fault.
- The IHT receipt for the tax will be submitted with the Will (if any) and the Oath, to the Probate Registry with the requisite fees https://www.gov.uk/wills-probate-inheritance/applying-for-a-grant-of-representation

If no IHT is payable

- A simpler IHT form is required – the **IHT 205** https://www. gov.uk/government/publications/inheritance-tax-return-of-estate-information-iht205-2011
- Once it is completed the IHT 205 itself is submitted with the Will and fee to the Probate Registry – this will have saved time, as there is no waiting for the IHT receipt from HMRC

Your probate practitioner will be able to advise you whether a Grant is required in a particular estate. When you do need a Grant, several copies are usually obtained to facilitate the efficient processing of the next stage.

The Probate Service handles other probate court procedures which may or may not be needed in a particular estate but it does not deal with disputes. These have to be made to the High Court (see Chapter 12) and can delay the administration of the estate considerably.

D. Winding up the Estate

The last stage of administration gets underway with the receipt of the Grant by the PRs from the Probate Registry. It is used to cash in the estate assets the proceeds of which will be used to settle all the debts and legacies. Some of the gifts under the Will may be specific, such as a gift of jewellery or pieces of furniture or particular shares. Also, there may only be one beneficiary e.g. you, and you may wish to have ownership of the deceased's property and not sell it. So the probate practitioner should discuss with the PRs and beneficiaries whether any assets which are not needed for the settlement of liabilities might be transferred to particular beneficiaries intact.

Depending on this review of the settlement of the estate and meeting the wishes of the deceased under the Will or the rules laid down by law in the absence of a Will, the probate practitioner will collect, sell or transfer the Assets.

To facilitate this the PRs sign withdrawal forms for any accounts and on receipt of funds the practitioner will use the proceeds to pay the liabilities and any legacies.

This process again may take many weeks depending on the complexity of assets in the estate and the speed with which third parties deal with the process of encashment. Where there is a property to sell the whole process may take many months whilst the property is cleared and sold.

However, no sensible PR and no regulated probate practitioner will distribute the estate without being certain that:

• The necessary time limits to protect them from claims have been followed i.e. if the statutory notices have been placed in the newspaper and the London Gazette calling for notice of any outstanding claims, you need to wait for two months from the date of the notice to gain its protection from personal liability against settling unknown claims

• All the known debts and liabilities and any loans to meet the IHT bill have been settled or sufficient cash funds are on deposit to meet them

• All taxes due have been paid or they are agreed and sufficient cash funds are on deposit to pay them by the due date – this is not always easy as income tax, in particular, can take some time to finalise and may only be for small amounts of adjustment

• There have been no claims made under the Inheritance (Provision for Family and Dependants) Act 1975 within six months of the date of the Grant being issued; although it is prudent to wait 10 months from the date of the Grant to allow the permitted time for service of the claim

• You have not been put on notice of any intended probate action such as a challenge to the Will or the ownership of assets, which threat has not yet materialised. There is no time limit on issuing these types of proceedings. Depending on the circumstances of a particular case, you may need a court order to protect you from personal liability

As part of the process of finalising the estate it is the duty of PRs to prepare Estate Accounts to demonstrate how the estate has been handled. Whilst there is a duty to account to the residuary beneficiaries there is no particular format as to how the accounts should be prepared.

The usual elements include:

* **An Introduction** – summarising the terms of the Will or the intestacy rules and who has administered the estate, the date of the Grant and other useful information to help understand the accounts
* **A summary of the Estate at death** – this could be in the form of a balance sheet
* **A Capital account** showing any capital assets; plus profits or losses on realisation and any capital taxes paid
* **An Income account** showing the income received for each tax year of the administration and any income tax paid
* **Distribution accounts** – which reveal who received what from the estate
* **Separate schedules** – are often added to simplify the capital and income accounts e.g. if the deceased owned a portfolio of stocks and shares there is likely to be a schedule of dividends received the total of which would appear in the income account
* **Additional notes** – may be added to explain particular items – such as how rental income has been dealt with or provision made for some unresolved item

Once draft accounts have been approved by the PRs then any remaining assets, which have not yet been distributed, are distributed according to the law, usually taking into account the beneficiaries' wishes, where possible. This may not always be possible if, for example, more than one beneficiary shares the residue and they cannot agree on how particular items are to be dealt with. In the end the PRs word is usually final and they must sell the item for the best possible price in the open market. The beneficiaries will be free to bid for them.

Any assets that are not being realised but are being retained by the relevant beneficiary must have the legal title to the assets appropriately transferred to them e.g. a property will have to be conveyed to the beneficiary and the title registered at HM Land Registry.

The probate practitioner on closing their file should consider which documents belong to the PRs or beneficiaries and return them. Otherwise, they will archive their file. A regulated probate practitioner must comply with their regulator's requirements in this respect.

Many regulated providers will offer to store important documents – if as beneficiary you wish them to do so ensure they have updated their records and databases so nobody writes to the deceased about them in the future instead of you.

6.5 Checklist

* Decide whether you are able to undertake the whole estate administration yourself or not – you may be too upset at the deceased's death or not up to the paperwork
* If you are not going to undertake the work yourself ask a regulated probate practitioner to do it for you. See paragraph 5.5 in Chapter 5 for tips on choosing the right sort of practitioner for you
* Collect together the financial records of the deceased to hand over to the registered practitioner – ask them for a checklist to help you
* Take your Money Laundering identification evidence with you when you go to the first meeting with your regulated probate practitioner
* Ensure you obtain a written quote or estimate for the costs and extra payments likely to be incurred in the estate administration
* If you are going to undertake part of the process yourself but need the regulated probate provider to undertake the rest then be sure it is clearly agreed in writing what s/he will and will not be doing for the fee agreed
* Agree a reporting strategy for progress with the regulated probate provider – e.g. ask for a monthly update by e-mail and for any explanations where something is taking longer than the average
* Help with some tasks to keep the costs down, such as visiting an empty property, as required by the insurance company, if you are sufficiently local to it
* Question anything you do not understand rather than suffer in silence

Chapter 7: What you need to know to get the best out of lawyers who help you to mitigate tax on death

Inheritance Tax (IHT) is probably one of the UK's most hated taxes. You might see it as a tax on your hard earned savings on which income tax has been paid already. Whilst it is not exclusively paid on death (there are special occasions in relation to trusts where it has to be paid) its origins are a duty paid on death.

It differs from a wealth tax, common in other countries, because in the UK IHT is charged on the value of the estate of a deceased person on death and not exclusively on the recipients' personal wealth.

Over the past 20 years IHT has been tinkered with and altered in such a way that the tax is something of a mess to explain and administer. There have been a number of proposals for its reform including: abolishing the tax, taxing the recipients rather than the deceased's estate and increasing the threshold of the starting point for paying the tax. At the time of writing this book it is under review again.

Recently, it has become more of a contributor to the nation's tax take, largely due to the inflation in house prices. In 2015/16 it raised £4.7 billion and the Office of Budget Responsibility, *Economic & Fiscal Outlook* for March 2017 estimated that the forecast receipts for 2017/18 will be £5 billion. HMRC estimate that it is payable on about 4% of all estates.

It is by no means certain that you will be one of the 4% but this Chapter aims to explain how the tax is structured and to show you the record-keeping you need to undertake to help your adviser help you. Hopefully you will understand IHT's impact on your estate and what, if anything, you can do to ensure your estate pays only a fair contribution.

In February 2018 the government asked the Office of Tax

Simplification to review IHT. This may result in changes to the tax or even its abolition. What follows is the law as at 1 February 2018.

7.1 Structure of IHT

IHT may be charged on certain lifetime gifts, e.g. on a transfer of assets into a discretionary trust, certain transfers into and out of trusts; but also on the value of your estate at the time of your death.

All UK domiciled individuals are chargeable to IHT on **all** their worldwide property. Non UK domiciled individuals are chargeable to IHT in respect of their UK property only. "Domiciled" under the common law largely means the place you regard as your permanent home. There is however an extended meaning for IHT purposes. You are deemed to be UK domiciled if:

- You were born in the UK with a UK domicile of origin but obtained a domicile of choice elsewhere and have returned to the UK and become UK resident; or
- You have been resident in the UK for at least 15 out of the previous 20 years

Spouses and civil partners are chargeable separately so each can make full use of individual exemptions and reliefs. Provided both are domiciled or deemed domiciled in a UK country then gifts between you are exempt. Otherwise, special rules apply.

The tax is **chronological and cumulative** so you need to keep a record of your running total of your lifetime transfers. The cumulative total of lifetime gifts is only relevant for **seven years** prior to death. Transfers are usually excluded from the running total outside that period.

Once the total of lifetime transfers coupled with the value of your estate on death exceeds the 0% tax threshold then tax is chargeable on the excess at the rate of 40% (death rate) and 20% (lifetime rate), unless the reduced rate of IHT (36%) applies because of the level of your charitable giving – see https://www.moneyadviceservice.org.uk/en/articles/the-tax-benefits-of-giving-to-charity.

The value of the 0% band is known as the **Nil Rate Band (NRB)** for the obvious reason that the rate of tax on that band of value is

0%. It is important to note that it is not an exemption but a 0% rate of tax.

An unused NRB can be transferred between spouses and civil partners at the rate applicable on the second death. Thus, when the NRB is £325,000, if all your spouse's estate is given to you on death there will be no tax due as that gift is exempt. As a result 100% of your spouse's NRB remains unused and is available to carry forward to you. On your death you will be entitled to your own NRB plus in addition a transferred NRB (TNRB) valued at 100% of the NRB applicable at your death i.e. £650,000 will be subject to the 0% rate of tax.

To the NRB and the TNRB has been added a further extension, which relates only to residential property – the **Residence Nil Rate Band** (RNRB). This applies where you own a qualifying residential property (e.g. your home) in your estate on death and transfer it to a lineal descendant (e.g. your son).

There are some complex rules affecting its application see https://www.gov.uk/guidance/inheritance-tax-residence-nil-rate-band but it adds a further £100,000 (2017/18) to the NRB upon which no IHT is payable. This RNRB rises by £25,000 each tax year until 2020/21 when it reaches its maximum of £175,000.

Each spouse or civil partner is potentially entitled to a RNRB if the conditions are met and again unused RNRBs may be transferred between spouses and civil partners. This means that by 2020/21 a further £350,000 of value could be transferred on the second death to say, your children, without IHT being charged – that would mean a total of £1 million of value would be IHT free across the two estates of a married couple or civil partners but *not* cohabitants or others living together, such as siblings.

Potentially exempt transfers (PETS) – these are lifetime transfers upon which no tax is payable at the time that they are made instead we wait and see whether or not you die within seven years. Even so, there will be no tax to pay on them unless the total of all your PETS exceeds the NRB threshold applicable on the date of your death. Failed PETs (i.e. those made within seven years of your death) therefore reduce the amount of NRB threshold which is then available to set against the value of your estate on death.

A PET which becomes chargeable because of your death within seven years is brought into account at the value of the gift at the **time it was made** and the tax is calculated on the basis of the rates in force at the time of your death. For example, if you gave some shares worth £10,000 to your daughter and then died five years later when the shares were worth £15,000, the amount of the failed PET which would be treated as part of your estate on death would be £10,000 and not £15,000.

Chargeable lifetime transfers are transfers which are immediately chargeable when made and therefore could incur tax at the lifetime rate (20%). The main categories of such transfers are transfers to some trusts or some companies.

As with PETS, such lifetime chargeable transfers are taken into account in assessing the rate of tax on death. If death occurs within seven years of chargeable lifetime transfers having been made then tax is recalculated on those chargeable lifetime transfers at the full 40% rate. It may be appropriate to claim the value at the date of death instead if the value of the asset has fallen in the meantime.

The tax on chargeable lifetime transfers is usually paid by the recipient but if it is paid by you, as the transferor, then the amount of tax chargeable is found by a complex method called 'grossing up' – see https://www.gov.uk/guidance/work-out-what-part-of-your-estate-pays-inheritance-tax.

On death you are treated as making a final transfer of the whole of your estate immediately before death and the tax charged on your estate will depend upon the total of chargeable lifetime transfers and potentially exempt transfers within the previous 7 years.

Special rules apply when a chargeable transfer was made in the seven years prior to a PET which fails.

Exempt transfers – certain gifts are exempt from IHT irrespective of their size and whether made during your lifetime or on death:

- Gifts made to your spouse or civil partner – see above
- Gifts made to charity
- Gifts made to political parties

- Gifts made to certain special bodies in the national interest such as the British Museum, galleries, universities and other museums

There are also some gifts which you can make during lifetime, including the last seven years of your life, which are also exempt. The most common are:

- Gifts made in a specific tax year (i.e. 6 April to the following 5 April) not exceeding £3,000
- Any number of individual gifts to different people worth up to £250 – this is in addition to the £3,000 exemption but it cannot be added to it if made to a single person
- Gifts made as part of your normal expenditure out of income taking one year with another, which leave you still enjoying your usual standard of living. There must be a commitment to do this on a regular basis e.g. a covenant to pay your grandson an allowance of £5,000 per annum during his time at university.
- Gifts to certain family members in consideration of marriage

Gifts made which are not exempt may qualify as a PET.

There a number of other exemptions which may be relevant to you personally upon which you should seek specialist advice e.g. on divorce. There are also some particular reliefs which are valuable to farmers and business owners. These reliefs are called **Agricultural Property Relief** (APR) and **Business Property Relief** (BPR), respectively. Both are conditional on meeting a number of criteria and there has developed a substantial body of law around them as to when they do and do not apply which is outside the scope of this work. As the value of agricultural land and business assets may in some cases be reduced by as much as 100% if APR and/ or BPR applies (and so effectively make these assets exempt from IHT) specialist advice must be taken as to how and in what circumstances your assets will benefit from these reliefs.

Gifts with reservation of benefit (GROBs) – are where you make a disposal, which is a gift (that includes any sales at less than market value) but continue to enjoy the use of the property so transferred. Such a gift will be treated for IHT purposes as if its value still formed part of your estate e.g. you give your home to your daughter who does not live with you and you continue to live there without paying a proper rent to her for its use. The full market value of the property will be **deemed for IHT purposes** to still be in your estate on death, even though the gift was valid in law.

The effect of making a GROB is that:

- The recipient does own the asset the subject of the GROB so if s/he dies IHT may be payable on it as part of their estate
- If the GROB continues over the property until your death its value at the date of your death is treated as being still within your estate for IHT purposes
- If property ceases to be subject to a GROB before your death e.g. you move into a care home, you are deemed to have made a PET at the market value of the asset at that time
- There is no re-basing for capital gain tax (CGT) (which usually occurs on the death of a donor) even though the GROB means that IHT may be payable on the same value at that time. E.g. if you gift your house to your daughter when it is valued at £300,000 and continue to live in it until your death when it is valued at £400,000 then your estate pays IHT on your estate, including the house at £400,000; whilst your daughter, if she sells the house following your death, will also be subject to CGT on the difference between the sale price of £400,000 and £300,000, the value at which she acquired it, subject to CGT rules.
- The donee as the recipient of the gift is the person responsible for paying any IHT applying to that gift on your death as a result of the GROB rules. So in the example, your daughter would pay IHT on the £400,000 as the recipient of the gift and CGT on the chargeable gain of £100,000 without one tax being set off against the other. In other words, there is a prospect of double taxation.

Your estate on death therefore comprises:

- Any assets held jointly e.g. your home owned jointly with your spouse or civil partner
- Capital of any trust fund in which you enjoyed a qualifying interest in possession – see Chapter 9
- Any PET which now becomes chargeable
- The value of any assets over which a GROB applied at the time of your death

The value of your estate does not include the value of any **excluded property** i.e. property situated outside the UK, if you died domiciled outside the UK; or, any **reversionary interests** under a trust. Excluded property can therefore be transferred without any charge to IHT even if the transferor dies within 7 years of making the transfer. For example, if grandad gifts his property to grandma for life and then stipulates it goes to his son on her death, grandma has an interest in possession and the son has a reversionary interest. The son's reversionary interest is excluded property and he can gift that interest to the grandchildren whilst grandma is alive (but not afterwards) without any IHT consequences on the son's death.

Liabilities owed on death are in general deducted in determining the value of your estate on death e.g. any mortgage which may still be owed to a commercial lender. Some debts are not deductible and specialist advice will be needed about this.

Calculating the tax position on death is based on an account which your personal representatives (PRs) must deliver to the HMRC giving full details of your estate for IHT purposes – see Chapter 6.

IHT is payable within six months of the end of the month of death. The account must be delivered to Her Majesty's Revenue and Customs (HMRC) within 12 months of the end of the month in which you die or within 3 months beginning with the date when the PRs first acted as such, if later. There are penalties for failure to pay tax on time; failure to deliver an account on time and for making incorrect Returns.

7.2 How to identify if IHT affects you

First of all, list all your assets and liabilities (and if possible those of any spouse or civil partner) and attach a reasonably accurate valuation to each item. You will find a simple checklist at the end of this Chapter.

Some assets may be jointly owned such that the asset will automatically belong to the surviving co-owner on the first death. A common example of this is often the family home when the owners are married or civil partners. (For an explanation of the types of co-ownership of land see Chapter 1).

To help your chosen adviser explain the impact of IHT on your estates please check how you own your various assets as this will make a difference to the advice you receive. If you are not sure how you own some assets or are unclear of the type of ownership, ask your adviser to help you.

Largely, deducting the value of your liabilities from the value of your assets will leave you with your net estate value. Is this more or less than the current NRB?

If you undertake this exercise for both you and your spouse and civil partner it will provide some idea of the likely amount of value which you might be leaving on the second death (assuming you want to leave your estate to your surviving spouse or civil partner on the first death) to your chosen beneficiaries by your Wills or under the Intestacy Rules – see Chapter 3.

So if your total joint net estate is valued at £750,000 of which £400,000 is represented by the value of your house and you intend that all your estate will pass to your surviving spouse on your death and then on the survivor's death it will pass to your children equally, there will be no IHT due on your estate and none due on the survivor's estate because:

- The transfer of your estate to your spouse is exempt
- The transfer of a £750,000 estate to children will benefit from:
  - Your spouse's NRB – £325,000
  - Your unused and transferred NRB – £325,000
  - Your spouse's RNRB – say £175,000
  - Your unused and transferred RNRB – say £175,000

If your estate is more complicated e.g. it contains business assets; or, you and your partner are not married; or you have children from more than one relationship then the calculation will need to be undertaken by a specialist.

To assess the impact of IHT on your estate it is important to:

- Keep records of all gifts, transfers, acquisitions and disposals and their value at the time
- Identify your objectives in terms of providing for yourself, your spouse or civil partner and the rest of your family

- Be able to provide to your adviser a full list of your current assets and liabilities with their approximate values
- Record how you own your assets
- Identify any expected major changes to your position such as a forthcoming marriage; an inheritance from parents; the birth of a child or grandchild; retirement
- Seek independent financial advice on your circumstances – see https://www.moneyadviceservice.org.uk/en/articles/choosing-a-financial-adviser

Depending on the outcome of any advice you receive it will be prudent to make a Will, if you have not already done so, or review any existing Will to reflect your current wishes and changes in law and tax – see Chapter 3.

As part of planning what to do with your estate and minimising the impact of IHT you may be advised to create a trust – see Chapter 9 – either during your lifetime or in your Will.

7.3 Mitigating IHT

Reducing the likelihood or amount of a charge to IHT on your estate on death relies on being organised and realistic. Tax planning is allowed but increasingly changes in public opinion about tax planning are being reflected in tax rules which punish tax avoidance and also criminalise tax evasion.

Tax evasion is where you default or shy away from paying tax which is due. This is serious and can land you, and any adviser complicit in your evasion, in jail.

Tax avoidance is where you have stretched the terms of tax law to create a series of steps in a transaction for the sole or main reason of avoiding the payment of tax or increasing the eligibility for reliefs and exemptions or repayments of tax. This too is penalised.

Tax legislation requires creators of packaged schemes to reduce IHT to disclose them on creation and then anyone who uses them has to disclose they have done so on their next tax return. This may result in action being taken to close down the scheme or challenge its effectiveness. This is known as Disclosure of Tax Avoidance Schemes or DOTAS. https://www.gov.uk/government/publications/disclosure-of-tax-avoidance-schemes-inheritance-tax.

Plain vanilla tax planning remains permissible as long as it is conducted within the spirit of the law. For example, if the way your Will is drafted would mean you lost out on the RNRB then it is permissible to alter it to ensure your estate benefits from the RNRB.

As far as lifetime planning is concerned, explore all the lifetime exemptions and make sure, if you can afford it, that you utilise them. Unspent income is effectively capitalised and makes it more likely your estate will pay IHT on your death. As we get older we sometimes spend less on daily living because we have paid off our mortgage and might forgo a car, travel abroad less and give up gym membership. If you are in receipt of an indexed linked pension you may find that your income is going up but your spending is coming down and there is more unspent income which is accumulating in your bank account. Consider making annual exempt gifts totalling £3,000 to say, your children or bigger gifts, if you arrange to utilise the normal expenditure out of income relief.

If you have a serious amount of surplus cash and would like to reduce your estate so that what is left is within the NRB, TNRB and RNRB you could make an outright gift of it. It will be a PET to the extent that it exceeds the annual exemption. You just have to live seven years for it to drop off your cumulative total. If you are reluctant to provide £325,000 of assets to your young grandchildren, you could always put the money into a trust for them. This way you get the capital out of your estate (as long as you live seven years) and any growth in the value of the capital, through careful investment by the trustees, will belong to the trust and not affect your estate on death.

Making a significant dent in your IHT bill when you are worth more than £1 million will usually necessitate considering the type of assets you are invested in and whether there is any scope for changing them. For example, you may not have an interest in a business but your son and daughter have set one up in which they would like you to invest. Only invest if you can afford to lose the money but to the extent that the business is a trading entity you will have acquired a business asset entitled to BPR after you have owned it for two years.

Switching investments to a more risky type of investment is not appropriate or prudent for everyone and should only be done after you have obtained independent financial advice.

7.4 Finding a tax adviser

Tax advice is not a regulated legal service but nevertheless providers of tax advice include regulated professionals such as:

- Accountants www.icaew.co.uk
- Chartered Institute of Taxation members – https://www.tax.org.uk/homepage
- Solicitors http://solicitors.lawsociety.org.uk/?Pro=True
- Barristers https://www.barcouncil.org.uk/using-a-barrister/find-a-barrister/
- Independent Financial Advisers (IFAs) – https://www.fca.org.uk/firms/financial-advisers

When you are investigating how to mitigate your IHT bill on death you are seeking estate planning advice. This type of advice will often be ancillary to other actions e.g. your retirement from your business and so might be offered by your accountant; your retirement from employment and so will be reviewed by your IFA or it may be ancillary to making your Will since your Will might be drafted differently were it to take into account IHT mitigation and not simply succession to your estate and so will be reviewed by your solicitor.

7.5 Checklist

- Decide whether you need IHT planning advice or not by completing the Assets & Liabilities schedule.
- If you feel you would benefit from IHT planning advice, reflect on the right type of regulated practitioner to help you. It may be that your IHT planning needs are part of a retirement plan and so your IFA might be best; or, it might be part of a review of your Will, in which case a solicitor might be best. See paragraph 5.5 in Chapter 5 for tips on choosing the right sort of practitioner for you.
- Take your Money Laundering identification evidence with you when you go to the first meeting with your regulated practitioner.
- Ensure you obtain a written quote or estimate for the costs and extra payments likely to be incurred. For an IHT planning exercise it is likely to be an estimate of time spent at hourly rates which will be specified.
- Question anything you do not understand rather than suffer in silence.

ASSETS					
Item	Sole owner?	Joint owner?	Type of joint interest?	Value of Proportion	Value of Whole
Home					
Other Land/ buildings					
Personal Possess- ions					
Car					
Bank account					
Building Soc account					
BPR/APR					
Quoted shares					
Unquoted shares					
Unit Trusts/ Investment Trusts					
PEPS/ISAs					
Insurance policies (written in trust?)					
Life					
Pension					
Investment					

National Savings accounts					
Premium bonds					
Trust interest					

Item	Sole owner?	Joint owner?	Type of joint inter-est?	Value of Pro-portion	Value of Whole
Assets subject to general/ specific power of appt					
Lifetime gifts – to whom and when made					
Death in service provision?					
Nominat-ion of Death in service in favour of a recipient?					
Other					
Estimated Total Value					£ _____

Has the testator made promises to anyone that they are to receive any of these assets? Give details if so.			
LIABILITIES			
Type	**Secured/ Unsecured**	**Indemnity Ins.**	**Amount**
Mortgage			
Bank Overdraft			
Other			
Estimated Total Value			£ _____

Chapter 8: What you need to know to get the best out of lawyers who help you to plan the succession to your business

As with most other chapters in this book you need to do some thinking and background research to ensure a good outcome from your interaction with lawyers. In the case of succession to business many good ideas are provided by accountants. Take for example Deloitte's publication which is a compilation of a six-volume series that addresses the broad range of topics that business owners need to consider in order to facilitate an orderly transition of management and ownership https://www2.deloitte.com/content/dam/Deloitte/us/Documents/Deloitte%20Growth%20Enterprises/us-dges-business-succession-planning-collection.pdf or some tips from Price Waterhouse Coopers PwC – https://www.pwc.com/gx/en/family-business-services/publications/assets/pwc-10-important-points-when-considering-business-transition.pdf. Some law firms provide insight too – http://www.gannons.co.uk/expertise/shareholder-rights-solicitors/share-transactions/succession-planning or try https://social.luptonfawcett.com/blog/importance-succession-planning-family-businesses-good-bad-and-ugly.

It is a sad fact of business transitioning that most hand overs fail due to family disagreements or tax consequences. Family businesses are inevitably difficult because of the interaction between what is best for the business and what is best for the family.

Dealing with the succession to your business may be part of reviewing what happens to your estate on death. However, it could simply be that you want to retire or at least spend not quite so much time running your business. Whatever your objective, please remember planning the succession to your business is not your next big deal which has to be conducted quickly; it is about having a strategy for success to ensure the security of your family enterprise for what could be many years into the future and should be approached calmly and carefully.

To achieve such a strategy requires a detailed assessment of assets and liabilities, current and future needs both known and anticipated and an understanding of what will be personal family issues.

The key to success is to start to plan the succession early – as much as five years before you seek to retire. Here are a few tips to start you thinking before you instruct your lawyer.

8.1 What sort of business owner are you?

Business owners come in all shapes and sizes each with:

- **Different business ownership structures** for example, are you a sole trader; or, do you work in partnership with others; or, do you own shares in a company which runs the business?
- **Different operational points of view** – do you like to make all the decisions or do you delegate some decisions or work to employees or other partners or shareholders or directors in your company?
- **Different concerns about family life** – for example, do you have children and are they all happily married or in stable relationships? Or are you worried that a breakdown in family relations would mean a break up of your business?
- **Different visions for succession to and management of the business** – for example, would you only want family members to run your business or would you prefer to engage the best managers and have your family share the profits of the business?
- **Changing priorities at different points in life** – are you simply changing direction and need a new challenge so need to arrange for someone else to manage this business whilst you forge ahead with something new; or, are you looking to slow down and eventually retire?

As part of the succession process your lawyer will need to review your business documentation so it is worth making sure you have copies of:

- The title deeds or any lease of the business premises

- Your partnership agreement, if you operate as a partner in a partnership
- The Memorandum and Articles of Association of the company, if you are a shareholder of a company
- Any shareholders' agreement, which sets out in a private document what arrangements there might be between the shareholders over to whom and on what terms you are allowed to transfer shares
- Any cross option agreements between you and your co-owners over policies of insurance or other assets to deal with a sale or transfer between you
- Copies of the last three to five years of business accounts
- An inventory of assets comprised in the business, their nature and location. Try and compile one if it doesn't exist because any adviser or person getting involved in the business will need to understand what you own, what your spouse or civil partner owns and what third parties may own who may have to agree to your plans
- Identify digital assets too and review those which relate to the business and those which are personal

For some of you, succession planning might end up being planning to sell. Do remember when thinking of your objectives (see 8.2) that you and your spouse or civil partner will need to maintain a certain standard of living after you have parted with your interest in the whole or part of your business. Can you afford to do that or should you sell up and invest the proceeds in a decent pension?

If you have not up to now involved your family in the business how will they suddenly get the hang of running it? If your future financial security is partly going to be based on receiving dividend income from the shares you might retain in the business or rental income from renting premises you own to the business that business needs to thrive after you are no longer involved. Will it do that if you have not involved your family in the discussions and planning about your retirement?

You will need to listen carefully to your chosen family members. What are their goals? What are they worried about? For example, they may be used to being employed and receiving a monthly salary cheque and would find it hard to move to only taking remuneration when the business could afford it. What skills do they have? Some of them may have totally inappropriate skills whilst others might be interested in developing them if they are not yet up to speed.

In many cases family members may already be working in the business and have an expectation that they will inherit the business on your retirement or death. However, it is not usually the case that all children work in the business and even if they do they may be itching for a chance to stop and do something else.

Choose an adviser who, rather like the cases studies on the old TV programme 'Can't Take it With You', will encourage you to discuss the process of succession openly and fully with your children so that the risk of relying on untested presumptions is minimised.

Such a discussion could not only address succession to the ownership but also whether there should be a special business executor in your Will. It might also assist the child who is intended to take over the business, to understand why you did what you did, where the gift might fall short of an outright gift. This might be because there are insufficient other assets in your estate to make a fair or appropriate gift to other beneficiaries. Therefore, consideration will have to be given to including in your Will preferential options to purchase for the particular 'heir apparent' rather than an outright gift, the proceeds of sale of which when exercised would help to fund other legacies.

In the Fifth episode of 'Can't Take it With You' the programme looked at two family businesses:

"Nev and Alan built up a £3 million business which son Damian wants them to leave protected for future generations. But daughter Vashti would like the freedom to decide what to do with her share of the business. Now, Nev and Alan have to face up to the fact that they may not trust their daughter to do what they regard as the right thing and preserve the business, but rather she would seek to sell her share.

Hans and Anna are in despair over how to hand on their £4 million garden-nursery business to their six adult children, three of whom disagree over who should take charge in the future."

Family business succession is never going to be easy but an experienced facilitator could help you make a winning transition.

8.2 What are you seeking to achieve?

A. You need to identify a clear vision, set of goals and objectives for the future of your business. You also need to be honest with yourself about what you need in retirement. Write down some ideas.

B. You need to select as your team of advisers not just people you can work with but advisers your successors can relate to as well. It is likely that in building your business you have already a professional team around you comprising an accountant and a lawyer amongst others. Sometimes it is the accountant who provides tax related advice over and above core accounting skills. However, solicitors and barristers too can do so. A winning combination of an accountant and a lawyer will work best as they often specialise in different taxes which would be relevant to your plans and lawyers can review and draft any changes to your business documents; whilst the accountant will help with the financial advice for the transition and beyond.

C. Set a realistic timetable for the succession plan to become fully operational – your advisers will be able to help you with this. For example, it might work best if you gradually work part-time for say three years and take your capital out over the same period, assuming you could afford to do that, before retiring completely.

D. If you are able to agree a succession to the next generation then include in the plan relevant learning and development for the people who are taking on new roles. Some of this may need next generation training to be supplied by your professional advisers and not just yourself and your staff in the business. Other organisations could help here such as the Confederation of British Industry (CBI) see http://www.cbi.org.uk/executive-development or the Institute of Directors https://www.iod.com/training. You could also find something local through your Chamber of Commerce. To see which Chamber covers your area look at the British Chambers of Commerce website http://www.britishchambers.org.uk.

E. Decide on how you will deal with any disputes between you and your family members along the way. This may seem harsh but emotions can run high and it is better to identify in advance that this could happen so that you have a better means of resolving the issue than falling out, possibly permanently. For example, agree that mediation would be used rather than resorting to taking legal action or breaking off relations. Whatever method you decide be sure to document this in your succession plan.

F. Take advice about the value of your business and the impact of taxation on any changes of ownership. How will this leave your spouse or civil partner in the event that you die during the period of the implementation of the succession plan?

G. Consider any deal breakers such that succession within the family will not be achieved and you have to decide to sell it instead. You will need to take advice on the options you might have to sell the business and the possibly different tax implications this may incur.

8.3 What sort of help might you need?
It will help if your chosen professionals have an interest in your business or at least the sector in which you operate. For example, if you run a hotel someone who has advised other hoteliers or others in the hospitality industry may have relevant understanding about property and tax issues relating to that sector e.g. https://www.josiahhincks.co.uk/sectors/hotels-leisure.

You may be a descendant of the founder of the family business and there are particular concerns about how artefacts and any collections made might be dealt with e.g. http://www.telegraph.co.uk/culture/9005001/Wedgwoods-fight-to-preserve-their-family-history.html.

Some assets, such as intellectual property rights (that is the right to use an image or an invention or a process designed by your business) will need expert advice to determine the best way to protect, exploit and hold them.

It will be clear from this that part of the job of the lawyer who will help you is to establish where the wealth is and who is entitled to exploit it and pass it on. It makes sense to choose people who can collaborate appropriately and work as part of a team to avoid fees being duplicated by different people doing the same or overlapping tasks.

There are online directories which can sometimes help you pinpoint a suitable person see http://smallbusiness.findlaw.com/closing-a-business/succession-planning-for-small-businesses.html.

8.4 Are you also making a Will?

Frequently, if not always, thoughts of retirement will mean it is time to consider end of life planning too. For more on making Wills see Chapter 3. Some tax reliefs apply on death but not during lifetime and vice versa. So it is worthwhile considering what might happen to your plans if you were to die. Be clear what objectives your partner in marriage or civil partnership has for the near and longer term as well, in particular, in relation to any share they may have in the family's assets. Lifetime giving may lead to significant savings of tax overall once you are both satisfied that family needs are secured.

If your business has been successful you will hopefully have used some of your income to invest in a pension. For many people most of their wealth may not be part of their taxable estate on death – it will be held in a pension fund and in real property owned as joint tenants with a spouse or civil partner. The existence of a good pension may be sufficient to fund your retirement without worrying about selling your interest in your business so you may be able to afford as a couple to gift your business interests to the next generation.

In the case of pensions, you can nominate who is to benefit from your fund if there is any left on your death. You will need to consider who will benefit from the fund if no nomination is made and what effect a nomination will have. An appropriate nomination may provide an IHT free pension fund for your children, if your surviving spouse or civil partner is already provided for or if you have no surviving spouse or civil partner.

8.5 Key benefits of selecting the right adviser

* The right adviser will be clear about the extent of the retainer they need to help you and the appropriate level of involvement with the family in general.
* The right adviser should instil confidence in you and the family to share all the information needed to help you reach the right conclusion.
* The right adviser will apply common sense to the situation as well as full knowledge of the requirements of Business Property Relief for Inheritance Tax, Entrepreneur's Relief for

Capital Gains Tax and as a firm be able to supply appropriate trust law, commercial law and contract law.

- The right adviser will help you avoid dissipation of your assets – conflicts within the family cause waste. The involvement of an independent facilitator in family discussions should prove vital in keeping things objective and neutral.

Finding the right adviser in this area is as much of a challenge as in other areas. Regulated providers would include accountants for business and tax work https://www.icaew.com/about-icaew/find-a-chartered-accountant and solicitors for legal and tax work http://solicitors.lawsociety.org.uk. Sometimes a barrister might be able to help with some of the specialist advice such as intellectual property rights.

Accountants, solicitors and barristers can belong to the Society of Trusts and Estate Practitioners (STEP) and whilst this is predominantly for trust and estate planners, as the name suggests, they often are familiar with acting in relation to the succession to a business. You can find more information about STEP members here https://www.step.org/for-the-public.

The Law Society will help you find a solicitor in your area who would have the relevant expertise to help you. There is a free service for those starting in business which can be found at http://www.lawsociety.org.uk/For-the-public/Common-legal-issues/Setting-up-a-business/Lawyers-For-Your-Business but a call to a solicitor offering these services would establish what fee paying services they offer for existing businesses.

8.6 Checklist

- Make that list of goals mentioned in 8.2.
- Discuss with your spouse or civil partner (if any) the impact on them as well of any change in the ownership and management of the business.
- Collect together all the relevant business documentation mentioned in 8.1.
- Arrange a joint discussion with your accountant, your lawyer and any IFA (regarding the pension side) about the plans you set out in 8.2. Ask them for their initial views about what will be involved and the costs and taxes you may have to budget for.

- Ensure you obtain a written quote or estimate for the costs and extra payments likely to be incurred in the process from each of your advisers and how they will ensure that they will work together without duplication of effort.
- Consider what part of the process you are going to undertake yourself and agree some staging posts as to what has to be done before the next stage can be tackled or what has to be done in tandem. Be sure it is clearly agreed in writing what any paid adviser will and will not be doing for the fee agreed.
- Decide at what stage you need to involve your family members or potential successors to your business in the discussions and plans and invite them along. Consider if you are likely to need an independent person, such as your accountant or solicitor, to act as facilitator.
- Agree a reporting strategy for progress – e.g. six monthly updates – to keep the momentum going.
- Encourage your potential successors to question anything they do not understand rather than suffer in silence; try and keep open to their ideas and listen to their concerns.
- Decide on any training programme which will ease your successors into place.
- Do not forget your staff and ensure you involve them in the process of transitioning your departure from the business.

Chapter 9: What you need to know to get the best out of lawyers who help you to understand your family trust

9.1 What is a trust?

A trust may be created expressly during your lifetime or may be included in your Will so that it operates from death; or, it may arise by operation of law (which means trust terms are implied); or, as a result of the courts assessing the behaviour of a person towards some or all of their property or that of another person (resulting or constructive trusts – this arises where the courts are dealing with the division of assets on the breakdown of a cohabitation relationship). There are special cases such as protective trusts, trusts created for disabled persons, trusts directed by court order as a result of personal injury claims, pension trusts, charitable trusts – indeed, trusts of all sorts exist in England & Wales.

The trust practitioner is often asked to explain the essential nature of a trust to clients. It is also necessary to be able to determine whether or not a particular gift or document has in fact created a trust.

A simple way of describing a trust is to say it is a 'gift with strings attached', but in law, for a trust to exist three certainties must be present:

- Certainty of words – A trust is a clear obligation imposed by its creator (the settlor) upon a person or persons (the trustees)
- Certainty of subject matter – To manage property under the trustees' control (trust property)
- Certainty of objects – For the benefit of the persons (the beneficiaries) whose interests are protected by the courts

The trustees are not personally the owners of the trust property. They are simply the custodians of that property appointed by the settlor to manage it for the benefit of the settlor's chosen beneficiaries.

117

To the outside world, and in fact, the trustees are the legal owners of the assets held in trust. However, they do not own the monetary value of the assets (known as the equitable interest in the property). Indeed, there are rules which enable beneficiaries to enforce in the courts, the terms of the trust against misbehaviour by the trustees so as to protect the beneficiaries' interests.

9.2 Where do trusts come from?

The trust concept is a unique creation of English law and has been spread around the world. It combines a number of historic points:

- The idea of a fiduciary holding assets for the benefit of someone else was Roman – they often appointed a friend to look after their assets on behalf of their children under a Will – but the Roman concept could only be used in Wills; whereas the English trust can be created as above.
- The idea that some of your estate must be used for the good of Allah even though under your personal control is a Muslim concept and similar to a charitable trust under English law.
- In the 12th Century, English land law only provided for a legal owner of land. During the Crusades, without the land being worked it would fall into ruin and an absent crusader still had to pay his feudal dues to the Lord of the Manor. So he transferred the land to someone else to farm whilst he was away 'on the understanding' that it would be returned to his ownership on his return.

  Sadly, many crusaders discovered that the person to whom they had transferred the land was unwilling to return it to them. Their only recourse was to petition the King and he received so many petitions that he delegated dealing with them to his Chancellor of the Exchequer. Under this system instead of looking at who was legally the owner, the Chancellor looked at what was fair and equitable. In many cases he found in favour of the crusader who then benefited from the financial returns even if someone else used and legally owned the land.
- The idea of upholding fairness and equity developed as a separate set of rules in the Courts of Equity (see chapter 12) until these courts were combined with the other courts in the 19th Century. Certain remedies in court are to this day seen as equitable remedies.
- Despite Henry VIII trying to abolish 'Uses', as they became known, he had to compromise and agree to permit those uses

where there was active management of the assets. From that day to this Uses or Trusts, as we call them to-day, have been a significant tool in the management of family assets.

9.3 Why create a trust?

9.3.1 To protect assets

Families may have worked for generations to create a business, a farming enterprise or to manage a landed estate and desire to protect these assets from any future unfortunate liaisons, poor business decisions and spendthrifts.

At the other end of the spectrum, even if there are no substantial assets involved, just a reasonable nest egg for the family, parents may very well wish to ensure that these assets are preserved as such, because otherwise they fear that they will be dissipated sooner rather than later. (For example, they may have a son or daughter with an addiction which impairs their ability to make sensible use of the assets.)

In many ways, the protection or preservation of the assets will be necessary if the funds are to provide assistance to more than one group of beneficiaries. The obvious dilemma for many people is how to ensure that funds that are needed by a surviving spouse or civil partner will be preserved for their children once that surviving partner or spouse has formed a new relationship or subsequently passed away.

To answer your concerns about protection of the assets for your chosen beneficiaries a trust practitioner needs to be able to explain the opportunity afforded by an appropriate express trust over the seemingly attractive 'simple' approach of relying on everyone to act as you would have done if you were alive to deal with it – which runs the inherent risk that this is not what happens.

9.3.2 To protect the beneficiaries

Some people believe that their offspring will never know best and would love to protect their hard-earned savings from wastrel children. Equally, the inheritance may be devalued by division between siblings.

Trusts cannot prevent people making poor choices of life partner or remove the risk of funds falling in value during harsh economic times, but they can provide, in the form of trustees, a set of skilled people who are able to take reasonable decisions to protect the fund; to refuse inappropriate requests by beneficiaries for money or other resources and to generally take the needs of all beneficiaries into account not just those who shout the loudest.

You may have children with learning disabilities who will never be able to manage their own resources. If so, it is likely that you may worry what can be done, when both parents have died, to protect your children from unfortunate 'friends' and 'carers' who may not be all they appear to be. Trustees of a trust can act as a benign parent would have hoped to have done if they had lived, and provide special resources to make the beneficiary's life more enjoyable without losing the underlying basic care provided by public funding.

You may have perfectly able-bodied children who have sadly become addicted to drugs or alcohol to such an extent that providing a large sum of money to them as an outright gift would endanger their lives. Instead, you might prefer your assets to be managed for their benefit by someone who will provide a roof over their head, which the child cannot sell, so at least the child is safe, in the hope that the addiction problems might be overcome and your child survive to enjoy a healthy and happy later life.

Express trusts provide those of you who feel the need to protect your beneficiaries with a suitable tool to protect your chosen beneficiaries from, effectively, themselves!

9.3.3 To retain control over assets and beneficiaries by setting out the terms of use in the trust deed

The ability to transfer assets out of personal ownership but still effectively to dictate their use will be attractive to some of you. A gift could be made during your lifetime, rather than on your death, to a trust where you are one of the trustees. In that way, as a trustee, you can exercise control over the trust fund, although of course you must act entirely in accordance with the trust deed and in the best interests of the beneficiaries, not for your own benefit.

Alternatively, you can create a trust under your Will so that control beyond the grave is achieved in as much as the people given the job of managing the fund are those chosen by you. The chosen trustees are also directed by your Will to manage the assets as required by you for the circumstances you specified, so you can say who is to receive any income arising on the fund and/or what capital can be paid to them.

In the case of a family company, you may not wish to see the company broken up by a piecemeal division of the shares between your children or other beneficiaries. Putting the shares into trust would enable the company to remain intact and be sold as one entity yet meanwhile permit your chosen beneficiaries to enjoy the success of the company either in the form of dividends or ultimately by sharing in the capital value on its sale. The trust will prevent any one beneficiary from having control over the day-to-day business of the company. A trust is a popular mechanism for holding shares in a family business to achieve these objectives.

9.3.4 To treat income and capital of a gift in different ways

You will often have two main categories of people you wish to benefit – your surviving spouse or civil partner and your children. The spouse or partner may be financially dependent on you and would need access to your resources on your death to maintain a reasonable standard of living. However, if capital is given outright to your surviving spouse or partner this would leave them free to use it as they see fit. While this may be entirely satisfactory for some of you, others may have either more complex lives or less faith in the ability of their surviving spouse or partner to be able to manage those resources appropriately. By using a trust the income can be paid to the surviving spouse or partner while preserving the capital for your children.

Those of you who have been married before and have children from that relationship may expect to be able to preserve some or all of your estate for your children to benefit from, but if the estate is given directly and absolutely to a new partner there is no guarantee that any previous children would ever benefit.

You may have always managed the family's finances and may feel that your surviving spouse or partner would find the responsibility of managing money difficult. If so, you may prefer to ensure that there is sound management of the money by trustees, who would provide a suitable stream of income for your surviving spouse or partner.

In some cases you may have an elderly relative who needs help with the payment of outgoings and requires income to do this, but have no need of the capital that generates this income, which can be directed elsewhere on the death of that relative to other beneficiaries of your choosing.

Providing income for your children or grandchildren whilst they are too young to handle large amounts of capital is a popular use of trusts as they can provide funds for school fees, day-to-day maintenance and other benefits while the children are under a specified age. However, you may feel that at a certain age the children will be responsible enough to have control of their own funds, and the capital will usually pass to them on attaining that specified age.

9.3.5 To save tax

Trusts are also a way of helping to save capital taxes. For the couple who want to minimise inheritance tax (IHT) on their joint estates, the tax adviser would encourage making the most of various nil rate bands.

In the case of lifetime gifts, gifts into trusts up to the value of the nil rate band (see Chapter 7) are possible without incurring a charge to IHT at the time. Trusts may typically be used because your chosen beneficiaries are too young to enjoy the amount of cash outright and it needs to be managed until they reach a specified age. Nevertheless, you wish to reduce the capital value of your taxable estate on death and so need to make a gift sooner rather than later.

Another common situation in which to use a trust is where you do not have spare cash to give away but only have chargeable assets e.g. a holiday home; which, if given away, would generate a chargeable gain on which you would have to pay capital gains tax (CGT) at your marginal rate, which could be as much as 28 per cent. If the chargeable assets were gifted to a relevant property trust, for example, you could utilise a CGT relief to avoid an unwelcome tax bill.

9.3.6 To avoid the need to obtain a grant of probate

When an individual dies living permanently in England and Wales at their death, the legal title to their assets transfers to his or her personal representatives (PRs). To be able to provide evidence of the legal ownership a Grant of Representation must be issued to the PRs (see Chapter 6).

While in many estates this is straightforward, once the estate is taxable, accurate valuations are necessary and the PRs will have to undertake a reasonable amount of work to identify and value all the assets, liabilities and beneficiaries in the estate. All this takes time, and during this period assets cannot be easily changed or managed without a Grant.

Although there are procedures which will enable an expeditious grant to be obtained, even this is not instantaneous and could temporarily leave the beneficiaries without access to financial support.

Another factor may be the cost of obtaining probate. In 2017 the Government attempted but failed to significantly increase probate fees, such that estates worth more than £2 million would have to pay fees of £20,000 rather than £155 (for those Grants applied for by authorised probate practitioners or £215 if you do it yourself). With the snap Election in 2017 this proposed increase was withdrawn. It had been criticised not just for its scale but also for the manner of its introduction using the statutory instrument procedure rather than a Bill. These proposals may well be re-introduced at a later date.

The advantage of the trust is that the deceased is not the owner of the assets managed by the trustees. The trustees own the legal title to the assets in the trust fund and so are able to continue managing them following the deceased's death. This means that the trust's beneficiaries continue to have access to the support that they enjoyed before the donor's death, and more particularly the trustees have authority to switch investments as and when required, allowing them to react to the rises and falls of the markets.

9.4 Trust administration

Trusts need to be actively managed. You may have been asked to act as a trustee of a family trust and not be sure what is involved. Trustees have a fairly onerous task. They are obliged to follow the law and the terms of the trust document. Trust terms tend to be technical because of the need to be legally clear what was intended and to ensure the correct tax treatment. The taxation of trusts is complex.

It follows that you should not agree to be a trustee without being fully appraised of the terms of the trust, what it means and what it owns. You need to consider who benefits from it and whether you, acting as trustee, will be put in a position where your own position might be compromised through conflicts of interest – this is not uncommon in family situations particularly where a business or farm is involved.

You must also undertake due diligence to make sure there have been no breaches of trust by earlier trustees that need to be put right by them at their cost before you step into their shoes.

Whilst not all trusts are managed by regulated practitioners or trust corporations like Banks many are, on behalf of the trustees. Certainly, the more valuable the trust fund or the more complex the assets the greater the need for professionals to either act as trustees or to act as agents on behalf of the trustees.

Smaller trusts often arise under Wills and many High Street solicitors would be able to advise you on what needs to be done as part of concluding the estate administration of the deceased. Some of these trusts may not be needed on the deceased's death and can be closed down in some circumstances fairly easily.

Larger Will trusts or trusts which hold personal injury compensations or historic landed estates, businesses or farms etc, may need the services of a dedicated trust team. Larger solicitors firms; specialist accountancy firms or Trust Corporations are often needed here.

The best place to look for help with drafting and administering trusts of all kinds are members of the Society of Trust and Estate Practitioners (STEP) whose members specialise in the administration of trusts and estates – see https://www.step.org/ for-the-public.

Fees for drafting trusts in Wills or separate trusts created during your lifetime will usually be quoted for on an hourly rate; whereas, annual administrative charges are usually offered on a fixed fee basis which may be related to the value of assets under administration. Such a fee will normally cover dealing with trust registration, providing information to tax authorities including preparing the annual accounts and tax return and managing the investments. Fixed management charges will exclude exceptional items like buying and selling a property or dealing with a tax investigation. These sort of events will usually be quoted for separately when they arise.

Please note that the law requires that trust documents are prepared only by solicitors or barristers, a sensible precaution given they are regulated practitioners and trust drafting is a complex and potentially far-reaching task.

An additional administrative burden was introduced for trusts in 2017 – the need to register certain trusts on the Trust Registration Service – a digital register created and managed by HMRC. Its initial set up has been very fraught – see https://www.gov.uk/trusts-taxes/trustees-tax-responsibilities.

9.5 Different types of trust
There are a number of different types of trust regularly used in Wills and during lifetime by individuals. For an explanation of how they are taxed see https://www.gov.uk/trusts-taxes. These types of trust include:

9.5.1 Interest in possession trusts
An interest in possession trust is one under which a beneficiary has the immediate right to use or enjoy the property in the trust fund (for example, live in a house owned by the trust); or to receive any income arising from it, such as investment income or rents.

There are two different types:

* Those created on death and
* Those created during the lifetime of the creator (the settlor)

Those created on death are known as Immediate Post-death Interests or IPDI for short. Up to 22nd March 2006, all interest in possession trusts were treated for IHT purposes as owned by the person enjoying the interest in possession – called the Life Tenant. This treatment still continues for IPDI trusts.

But an interest in possession trust arising or created during lifetime on or after 22nd March 2006 will be taxed differently under a complex set of rules known as the **relevant property regime** – this means the fund is taxed on a periodic basis (every 10 years) rather than on the death of the life tenant and also when assets leave the trust, perhaps because the trustees have decided to appoint some capital or an asset to a beneficiary.

9.5.2 Discretionary trusts

Discretionary trusts are trusts where no beneficiary owns any part of the trust or has the right to direct the trustees to provide either income or capital to him from the trust. Instead, the trustees choose whose needs should be met and this may mean that no distributions are made in one year compared to another. It also means that unused income can be accumulated to the rest of the fund. They are highly flexible tools but more costly to administer and they are all subject to the complex relevant property regime rules for IHT.

Income tax rates are higher for discretionary trusts because of the ability to accumulate income. This is sometimes why powers to provide temporary rights to receive income are used to reduce the income tax charges.

9.5.3 Accumulation and Maintenance trusts – and their replacements

Accumulation and maintenance trusts were a special kind of hybrid arrangement which could benefit mostly young people under the age of 25. They were very popular until they were phased out following the IHT changes in 2006. Therefore, from that time no new ones can be made which enjoy a special IHT free status and old ones which continued, unless altered, fell into tax treatment under the relevant property regime for IHT.

The 2006 changes restricted tax saving trusts for children to children and step children who are bereaved and who benefit at either 18 (bereaved minor trusts) or at any age between 18 and 25 (Aged 18–25 trusts) under the Will or intestacy of their parent, step parent or person with parental responsibility for them.

Gifts made by others on death, such as grandparents and gifts you make into trust during your lifetime for your children or grandchildren where they have to reach a specified age to benefit will be subject to the IHT relevant property regime.

Depending on how trusts created during your lifetime are drafted and whether they exclude benefit for minor children or not they may be subject to special anti-avoidance rules for income tax and capital gains tax (known as the Settlor Interested Trust rules).

9.5.4 Disabled person's interests (DPI)

A DPI is a trust for the benefit of a disabled person. The disabled beneficiary will be treated on their death as if they own the trust assets for IHT purposes even though the terms of the trust do not give the disabled person an interest in possession. This means the relevant property regime for IHT will **not** apply while the disabled person is alive, nor on their death. Thereafter, it will depend on the terms of the trust.

A DPI created during your lifetime to benefit your disabled child say, is an exception to the rule that a lifetime trust is taxed as a relevant property trust for IHT. This means you can transfer as the settlor more than your available nil rate band of capital into the trust and it will not be immediately chargeable to IHT. It will be a potentially exempt transfer i.e. we wait and see if you survive seven years from making the gift – see Chapter 7. If you do then the gift into trust is ignored for IHT purposes when you die and you will have a fresh nil rate band available to set against your estate.

There are special conditions which apply e.g. if you make a discretionary trust for all your children, which includes your disabled son, then the trustees must use all distributions of capital or income for your son's benefit apart from £3,000 per annum (or 3% of the fund if less) which could be given to your other children. If these conditions are not met then the trust will not benefit from DPI status for tax.

9.5.5 Bare trusts

A bare trust is a trust whereby the trustees hold the legal title to an asset but the beneficiary is absolutely entitled to it. So for example, if in your Will you make an absolute gift of one third of your estate to your grand- daughter but she is only 10 at your death then she cannot under the law, provide a valid receipt to the PRs for this money. The money is hers but it will be managed until she is an adult i.e. 18 and can provide the necessary receipt for it. Although any income arising between your death and her attaining the age of 18, is her income and taxed as such, any capital also belongs to her and not the trustees. This means when she reaches 18 there will be no charge to IHT when the money is handed over yet meanwhile basic administration of the funds can be undertaken by your chosen PRs.

It differs from a contingent gift because you did not stipulate she must be 18, or any other age, before she could benefit from the money. You simply gave it to her unconditionally. If you do impose a contingent age then the tax treatment is different.

9.5.6 Asset Protection Trusts

An older and more vulnerable population is often concerned about losing their homes to meet the costs of their care. These concerns make older people easy prey for the unscrupulous to focus only on the benefits of so-called **Asset Protection Trusts (APTs)** to protect the value of a person's home from assessment to means tested benefits should the need for care arise, rather than take a more balanced approach.

They are not a separately taxed sort of trust but the name has stuck to cover a situation where a house is put into trust in the hope that it will not be taken into account for the purposes of assessing entitlement to means tested assistance with care costs.

Whilst there are some approaches which are entirely legitimate and where trusts can help in this situation the sector has attracted many unregulated providers who charge many thousands of pounds for 'products' which are not appropriate or cause more hardship than they purport to prevent.

For more on this topic see Chapter 10.

9.6 Checklist
* After reading the above if you would like to use a trust because the objectives you have for managing your assets now or on death make this the appropriate tool then consider the different motives in 9.3 above and the different types of trust in 9.5 before you select an appropriate adviser to help you finalise the best

arrangement – be that updating your Will or preparing a trust deed for you to operate now whilst you are alive.

- Remember that using a regulated practitioner is best – for drafting a trust it has to be a solicitor or a barrister.
- Share your objectives, thoughts and concerns with your chosen adviser and ensure they thoroughly explain the pros and cons of what you are trying to achieve and the taxation consequences, before you commit.
- Ensure you obtain a written quote or estimate for the costs likely to be incurred in either advising on the use of trusts for you and any drafting of the trust documents or administering the trust on behalf of the trustees.
- Make sure you have explored the tax consequences of creating the trust and transferring assets into it before you go ahead.
- Also, double check that you can afford to live without the assets you are transferring into the trust.
- You will be expected to produce identification evidence (such as a passport and a utility bill) to verify your identity and prove too the source of the assets which are to go into your trust.
- Always, check that the people you would like to act as trustees are willing to do so and have the appropriate skills. You may find this publication helpful in discussing the trustee's role with the people you would like to act as your trustees – https://www.step.org/sites/default/files/Comms/leaflets/Trusts_Explained_2016.pdf. Also encourage them to take a look at this website page – https://www.moneyadviceservice.org.uk/en/articles/being-a-trustee.

Chapter 10: What you need to know about the costs of care and how to help your lawyer advise you

10.1 The scale of the need for supported care

In August 2016, Prestige Nursing, one of the UK' biggest care agencies, highlighted that elderly people needing to go into care faced on average fees of £30,000 per year with costs rising 5.2% over the previous year. The Daily Telegraph at the time commented that this was almost ten times more than the average income earned by pensioners over the same period.

A major study published in the Lancet Public Health Journal, in 2017, predicted that the number of pensioners needing social care in the UK is set to rise by one quarter by 2025. As has been witnessed each winter in recent years, the number of people needing to be admitted to hospital on a daily basis outnumbered the spare hospital bed places due in large part to the number of elderly patients unable to find suitable care outside hospital.

Domiciliary care is care which is provided in a person's home and is often in the form of agency staff calling three or four times a day to help with getting the person up and to bed; washed; dressed and undressed; medicated as appropriate and fed. There is a strong wish amongst the elderly to be able to remain in their own home. Domiciliary care supports this goal but the demand outstrips the supply.

Where the level of care is such that living alone is too great a risk, perhaps because of the risk of falls or confusion causing injury, then often a move into a care home will be suggested by the Local Authority Social Services department. A care home provides social care rather than nursing care and ensures a person is supervised at all times. There are often activities organised for the residents to stimulate interaction and provide entertainment.

Some people need a higher level of care over and above basic support with everyday living. This may be because of illnesses like Alzheimer's disease or dementia. The Lancet research forecast a 40% rise in cases of dementia within a decade with the increasing number of older people living longer with the condition and with chronic diseases which require care. This type of care is often provided by nursing homes, which generally are more expensive than care homes.

The Competition and Markets Authority (CMA) identified in 2017 emerging concerns about the care homes sector. Their recent update report includes the following key findings:

- **Many people find it challenging to make decisions about choice of care** when under stressful & time pressured circumstances, such as an imminent discharge from hospital – particularly choices between social and health care. The CMA are exploring how better information and support could be provided.
- **Demand for care home services is fast outstripping supply**. The number of people aged 85 or over is projected to more than double by mid-2039 and the level of care needed is increasing as people are spending longer in their own homes before seeking a care place which means they are more frail when they do move to a care home – The CMA are considering how potential barriers to investment in the sector can be addressed and how it can be incentivised to invest for the future.
- **Building capacity takes time**. Recent financial performance of the sector overall is sufficient to cover current operating costs but insufficient overall to attract adequate investment in new care homes – where there are substantial self-funding people looking for places, investment in those areas looks more promising than those areas predominantly funded by Local Authorities.
- **Uncertainty over future funding of care is not helping to grow capacity** intended mainly to serve state-funded residents. These facilities have lower margins and it seems likely that this will not incentivise future investment.

The picture is bleak and different governments over the past ten years or more have delayed taking action. Some system of meeting the demand for and cost of care has to be found. The challenge is finding the right balance between state-funded-care and financing the cost privately.

10.2 What care is needed?

The Care Act 2014 sets out how a Local Authority (LA) must assess a person who requires care & support and the steps that must be followed to work out his or her entitlement; it imposes a general duty on a LA to promote an individual's **well-being** and for the first time requires LAs to assess any carer's needs.

'Well-being' is considered to mean:

- Personal dignity
- Physical & mental health & emotional well-being
- Protection from abuse & neglect
- Control by individual over day-to-day life
- Participation in work
- Social & economic well-being
- Domestic, family & personal relationships
- Suitability of living accommodation
- The individual's contribution to society

A needs assessment:

- Has to be given to all individuals who require care & support despite their financial position or whether the LA believes their needs are eligible – this is an essential first step which you should always ask for.
- Must be of the individual's care needs & consider how they impact on a person's well-being and take into account the outcomes that the person wants to achieve, such as remaining in their own home for longer.
- Has to be carried out with the involvement of the individual and their carer or someone else the person nominates.
- May involve an independent advocate if the individual requires it which should be provided by the LA to help with the assessment process.
- Must take into account other factors that can assist the person such as preventative services from local suppliers which might avoid the need to have care now e.g. some charities provide lunch clubs and transport.

The LA should consider the wider needs of the family. If you have capacity you can carry out a self-assessment – even though the LA is still involved to assist and ensure that you have highlighted all your needs. If the LA identify that you are eligible for NHS Continuing Healthcare the LA must refer you to the relevant body.

You will have eligible needs if:

1. You have care & support needs as a result of a physical and mental condition e.g. physical, mental, sensory, learning or cognitive disabilities or illnesses and brain injuries
2. As a result, your day to day outcomes are not achieved such as managing & maintaining nutrition, dressing, maintain personal hygiene and developing and maintaining family or other personal relationships
3. Because of 1 & 2 there is a significant impact on your well-being

The LA will provide a **Care & Support Plan** which must set out:

- Your needs
- The extent to which they meet the eligibility criteria
- The personal budget for you even if you do not want the LA to meet the care costs
- Any advice and information about what can be done to meet or reduce the needs in question
- What can be done to prevent or delay the development of needs for care & support

10.3 Paying for long-term care

There are three ways in which care of the elderly and vulnerable is paid for:

- By Local Authorities – this is known as **social care** and is subject to means-testing
- By the NHS – this is known as **NHS continuing healthcare** – this is currently provided free at the cost of the NHS
- By the person or their family paying for themselves – this is known as **self-funding** because the individual has to meet the costs from their own resources

This is a complex area and the charity sector offers useful advice e.g. https://www.ageuk.org.uk/globalassets/age-uk/documents/factsheets/fs10_paying_for_permanent_residential_care_fcs.pdf.

Although the Coalition Government appointed an independent Care & Support Commission to review the issue of sustainable funding for long-term care and the Law Commission undertook further work on reform of the law on adult social care, we are still without a satisfactory solution.

It is still the case that meeting the cost of care fees, when applicable, can mean the eventual loss of the family home. This concern drives poor decision making based on ignorance and fear. Whilst it is tempting to give away capital to your children, say, to ensure it is not all used up in paying for your care, do bear in mind that your children may not spend it wisely or may lose it through divorce or bankruptcy. Even if they were minded to help pay for your care they may by then be unable to do so.

The LA may have limited resources to pay for your care so even if you are eligible for their assistance the choice of care home may be limited and may not be to your liking. If you no longer have any resources to pay yourself you will be stuck with the place that is on offer. Your children may not offer or may not be able to offer, to top up the cost of a more palatable place.

10.3.1 The LA has a duty to carry out a financial assessment.
The details are contained in the Care & Support (Charging & Assessment of Resources) Regulations 2014 http://www.legislation. gov.uk/uksi/2014/2672/schedule/1/made (the Regulations).

Care which is free of charge

No charges may be levied for conducting the needs assessment, financial assessment and the care plan process	Creutzfield-Jakob disease sufferers are provided any services free of charge – Reg 4
Aids & minor adaptions that are required for intermediate care	NHS Continuing Healthcare
Re-enablement support services for the first 6 weeks – usually when an adult leaves hospital to return home	

Means testing is undertaken by the LA which must take into account Statutory Guidance supplied by the Department of Health https://www.gov.uk/government/publications/care-act-statutory-guidance/care-and-support-statutory-guidance.

Any capital (such as savings and investments) which is below the **lower capital limit** (LCL) is ignored. This is currently £14,250.

If your capital is £23,250 or above, the **upper capital limit** (UCL), then no financial support will be provided by the LA towards your care.

If your capital is between the LCL and the UCL then for every £250 above the LCL you will be assessed as having a £1 of income to help with the cost of your care.

Please remember that capital includes the value of your house or your interest in the house in which you live subject to detailed rules which may mean it is disregarded altogether.

LAs must regularly reassess your ability to meet the costs of any changes to your care plan as a result of changes to your resources. Each person is assessed individually – not as a unit e.g. in a married couple each spouse's resources are assessed separately.

What capital is disregarded in the financial assessment?

Schedule 2 of the Regulations and Annex B of the Statutory Guidance sets out the capital sums that must or may be disregarded by the LA. There is a long list of capital which must be disregarded in par 33 of Annex B in the Statutory Guidance https://www.gov.uk/government/publications/care-act-statutory-guidance/care-and-support-statutory-guidance#AnnexB.

The one topic which causes most people disquiet is the treatment of their home in the assessment process.

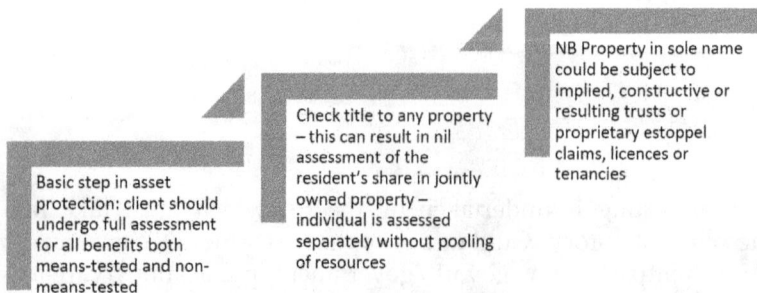

Basic step in asset protection: client should undergo full assessment for all benefits both means-tested and non-means-tested

Check title to any property – this can result in nil assessment of the resident's share in jointly owned property – individual is assessed separately without pooling of resources

NB Property in sole name could be subject to implied, constructive or resulting trusts or proprietary estoppel claims, licences or tenancies

The Statutory Guidance in Annex B par. 34 says:

A person's only or main home should be disregarded

- When receiving care in a setting that is not a care home e.g. domiciliary care at home.
- If the person's stay in the care home is temporary & they either intend to return to the property (and it is still available to them) or they are taking reasonable steps to dispose of the property in order to acquire a more suitable property to return e.g. Doris is awaiting discharge from hospital but needs to leave her three bedroomed house for a flat in a supported living development. The house sale is underway so the costs of a temporary move into a care home will not take into account her property which is in the process of sale.
- Where a person no longer occupies the property but it is occupied in whole or part by persons on the list who have been in occupation continuously since before the departure of the person to the care home e.g. Graham has moved permanently into a care home leaving behind his wife of 50 years, Frieda. She is aged 76 and still reasonably active. Their jointly owned home will not be taken into account in the financial assessment of Graham for the purposes of deciding whether the LA should pay for Graham's fees.

The list of persons who could be in occupation include:

- The person's partner, former partner or civil partner, unless estranged
- A lone parent who is the person's estranged or divorced partner
- A 'relative' of the person or the person's family who is either
  o Aged 60 or over
  o Is a child of the person aged under 18
  o Is incapacitated

For this purpose a 'relative' of a person includes:

- Spouses of all
- Parent
- Parent-in-law
- Son/daughter
- In-law

- Step parent/son/daughter
- Siblings
- Grandparent
- Grandchild
- Uncle/aunt/niece/nephew

The family home will be taken into account in the assessment process where the property is empty and not occupied by anyone now that its owner is living permanently in a care home; or, where the only people in occupation are not the spouse or partner of the person needing care and are aged over 18 and under 60 and not incapacitated, even if they were caring for the owner prior to his or her move into care. So if Andrew is a widower and moved out of his house which he shared with his son David, who is aged 50. Andrew's house would be taken into account in assessing his eligibility for financial support from the LA because David is his son and not incapacitated or aged under 18 or over 60.

Where a LA has decided to charge and has undertaken a financial assessment it should support you and try to identify the options of how best to pay for any charges. This could mean offering you a **deferred payment agreement**. LAs have to consider whether to enter into 'deferred payment arrangements' with you if you are a care home resident. The LA effectively lend money to you by paying the costs of your care for now without your home having to be sold in your lifetime to pay for it. Instead, the LA takes a charge on the house to protect their loan which is repayable following your death or earlier if the property is sold. More information can be found at:

https://www.moneyadviceservice.org.uk/en/articles/deferred-payment-agreements-for-long-term-care.

How is income assessed?

Income is treated differently depending on whether you are in a residential care setting or not. In a residential care setting only the income of the person being cared for is taken into account. When you are part of a couple it is presumed that both of you have an equal share in your income. The LA therefore has to take into account the impact this has on your partner.

Income is assessed net of any tax and National Insurance

contributions. All income is taken into account – pensions, annuities and most benefits, unless specifically stated to be disregarded.

Income that cannot be taken into account includes the following:

- Employed & self-employed earnings
- The mobility component of Disability Living Allowance & Personal Independence Payments
- Savings part of Pension Credit

When you receive support in other settings, rather than a care home e.g. domiciliary care at home, income is assessed differently:

- Other sources of income are taken into account although employment income is fully disregarded
- The rules say that you must have a **Minimum Guaranteed Income** (MIG) – this MIG ensures that an adult has sufficient funds to meet basic needs after paying the weekly care cost charges

10.3.2 NHS continuing care funding
Where a person's **primary need** is a health need the NHS is regarded as being responsible for providing for those needs, including accommodation, if that is part of the overall need. It is not available if nursing or other health services are **incidental or ancillary** to the provision of care and support services or if not of a nature beyond which the LA could be expected to provide.

In the January 2017 Health Service Journal, Disability United advised that at least 37 Clinical Commissioning Groups (CCGs) have imposed restrictions for adults with 'primary health needs' from accessing NHS continuing healthcare funding. Since the NHS spends around £2.5 billion each year funding continuing healthcare this is perhaps not surprising but it is a concern.

19 CCGs will not fund care in a person's own home if it is more than 10% above an alternative i.e. the cost of a care home. The remaining CCGs are imposing further restrictions to cut budgets.

This means that effectively the CCGs are shifting the burden of the costs of care to the social care system by contending that an adult's needs are not primarily medical. The winter crises in hospitals highlights the resulting problems with patients in hospital 'blocking beds' as they are not able to return home for lack of support.

This approach has a two- fold effect, it:

- Deprives a person of the right to live at home such as adults who have brain injuries or significant disabilities
- Burdens Local Authorities further with the costs of such adults' care

Challenging NHS continuing care funding decisions is difficult and time-consuming. There are some specialist solicitors who can help with this – try members of Solicitors for the Elderly.

10.4 Deliberate Deprivation of Capital

Probably the most controversial aspect of the whole care funding debate – If an asset has been transferred to a 3rd party to avoid the charge for care, the 3rd party can become liable to pay the LA the difference between what it would have charged and what it did charge for the care – limited to what they received from the transfer.

The test for deliberate deprivation of capital is one of **foreseeability & intention**. The LA has power to deem deliberately removed capital and income as notionally available when undertaking the financial assessment. The LA can potentially use the County Court process to pursue the debt.

The Statutory Guidance does acknowledge that there may be more than one purpose for disposing of a capital asset only one of which is to avoid a charge for accommodation. Avoiding the charge need not be the resident's main motive but it must be a significant one.

Timing of when a disposal took place does come into the equation. The Statutory Guidance says it would be unreasonable of a LA to decide that you had disposed of an asset in order to reduce your charge for accommodation when the disposal took place at a time when you are fit and healthy and the need for a move to residential accommodation was not foreseen. This is a difficult point. How easy is it going to be to show after the event that someone with early stage dementia or the start of Parkinson's disease will not need care in the future?

There is a difference between transfers made when there is the mere possibility of a need for care accommodation as opposed to undertaking a transfer when it is certain a move will be required.

Example

Elizabeth is a widow who now solely owns the matrimonial home. She is concerned about the prospect of needing care and the cost of that care since her diagnosis with dementia last month. She decides to transfer the ownership of her house to her son and daughter, neither of whom live with her. The property is worth £280,000. Two years later, after a nasty fall, it is clear Elizabeth cannot return from hospital to look after herself at home.

She is assessed by the LA to need a place in a care home. The LA is obliged to conduct a financial assessment and discovers the gift of her house to her children. The significant motive Elizabeth had at the time of the gift was to avoid the means testing assessment for the payment of future care fees. Although there was only a little expectation of the need for care at the time of the transfer, the gift was motivated by the desire to avoid paying for care. The value of the property will be taken into account as part of her capital, so making it necessary for her children to pay her care fees since they were the recipients of the gift of her property.

A failure to reimburse the LA for the costs of paying for Elizabeth's care can be recovered from the children through the courts if they fail to co-operate.

Annex E of the Statutory Guidance covers this issue – https://www.gov.uk/government/publications/care-act-statutory-guidance/care-and-support-statutory-guidance#AnnexE.

Annex D sets out the considerations for a LA when pursuing recovery of charges https://www.gov.uk/government/publications/care-act-statutory-guidance/care-and-support-statutory-guidance#AnnexD.

10.5 Asset Protection Trusts
Whilst all trusts are designed to protect assets (see Chapter 9) in the context of paying for care, it means the transfer of property to a trust (rather than make an outright gift to say your children) so that

the former owner can say they no longer own the property when it comes to financial assessment for means tested benefits – i.e. the house is not part of the capital of your estate as the applicant for financial assistance in the payment of care fees for you.

For example, a married couple Brian and Dawn co-own Sunny Bank as joint tenants. The property is currently valued at £300,000. This means they together own the whole value of the property and should one of them die the survivor will own the property outright.

When making their Wills it is pointed out that on the first death all the value of the property will pass to the survivor and this might not be in the family's best interests. Perhaps the first spouse to die would like to protect their interest in the house from any potential second marriage or from care home fees which the survivor may need to pay in future.

Brian and Dawn can change the way they own Sunny Banks so that they each own 50% of its value and can direct what happens to that in their respective Wills. This is known as tenants in common ownership and requires only a simple document to make the switch.

Brian and Dawn could then each make a Will in which they transfer their half share in the property to a trust which provides for the surviving spouse and their children Eric and Florence. If, say, Brian died first then half the value of the house would form part of his Will trust and not form part of Dawn's estate for the purpose of assessing her finances for care purposes.

Should Dawn need to go into care, her share of the proceeds of sale of Sunny Bank will be taken into account and will have to go towards her care costs; but once that capital is exhausted, or at least falls below the £14,250 lower capital limit, then the LA will have to reassess Dawn's financial position and start paying for her care instead. The LA will not be able to take into account Brian's trust fund.

This simple use of a trust in a Will is not controversial and an eminently sensible precaution to protect some of the family capital from care costs and second families.

However, there are more aggressive methods used by some to avoid future payments of care fees. These tend to be widely marketed by the unregulated sector as part of a bundle of services to include the making of Wills and LPAs as well. A solicitor advising on creating a lifetime settlement to avoid the future payment of care fees can face disciplinary problems as the act is likely to breach the Principles behind the SRA Code of Conduct 2011 (see Chapter 14).

In this method, use is made of a trust during the lifetime of the parties. Usually, the individual settles their house on trusts under which they retain a right of occupation. In the safer arrangements, the adult children will be the trustees. In more worrying cases the trustees will be members of the company selling the scheme.

The arrangements will always be vulnerable to a challenge by the LA should financial assessment arise because the significant motive in creating the trust, and making a gift of the property to it, was the deprivation of capital for the purpose of avoiding means testing for the payment of care fees. As explained above, this intention will enable the LA to treat the donor as still possessing the capital value given away and to pursue the recipients for the costs of care.

Also, when a lifetime gift is made there are rules in the Insolvency Act 1986 which enable a LA to set aside the gift if the making of it left the donor insolvent – which clearly it would do if he or she is unable to pay for their care due to insufficient resources. The Insolvency Act permits a creditor, here the LA, to go back indefinitely in time and set aside any gifts which placed the individual in this position. The transfer of the property into trust is such a gift.

To make matters worse, making a transfer into trust during your lifetime has tax implications – see Chapters 7 and 9. In cases where your house is valuable the arrangement would be positively unattractive for IHT purposes.

Some people are motivated by an irrational fear of the payment of care costs without thinking how cumbersome the alternative actually is – for some people using methods other than gifting the property to a trust during lifetime, to meet the payments, would be better; such as: letting the property out if needs be and using the rent, savings income and pensions to pay the care costs out of income, whilst retaining the capital asset, which is your property.

If you make a gift into trust when you are relatively young it may make it very awkward to downsize later. You will not own the sale proceeds on any sale, the trust fund will. You are not a beneficiary of the trust, your children are, so the trust fund cannot be used to buy your new property, unless the trustees agree to lend funds from the trust to you. This may not be possible given the terms of the trust.

Equally, if you still have a mortgage on your property it is unlikely that the mortgage lender will agree to the changes if it leaves you as the borrower with insufficient capital value in the property, which acts as security to meet the repayment of the mortgage.

In this area, almost more than any other, you need to seek the advice of a regulated practitioner particularly one who is familiar with these issues such as a member of Solicitors for the Elderly or a member of the Society of Trust and Estate practitioners.

For further information on this difficult topic see http://www.lawskills.co.uk/articles/2013/08/asset-protection-trusts-appropriate-or-dangerous.

And the Moneybox programme on Radio 4 entitled: Care Home Fees & the unregulated market http://www.lawskills.co.uk/articles/2017/05/care-home-fees-unregulated-market.

10.6 Other means of meeting the cost of care
10.6.1 Here are some choices for paying immediate bills:
- Pay out of savings & pensions
- Buy an immediate care annuity
- Use the Deferred Payment Agreement scheme
- Take out equity release on the house – see Chap. 16 Elderly Client Precedent Manual – 5th Edition – Caroline Bielanska – *Jordans*
- Let out the property
- Sell the property

10.6.2 Long Term Care Plans
If you plan ahead, long term care insurance can provide financial support. It can cover care in your own home or in a residential or care home. This is particularly helpful when you wish to make a significant gift to your family, perhaps for IHT planning purposes

(see Chapter 7). If you pay into a long term care insurance policy it can help protect that gift from a deprivation of assets challenge by demonstrating you have retained sufficient resources to pay for your care through the use of the policy funds.

Immediate care annuities pay a guaranteed income for life. They operate on the basis of you paying in a one-off lump sum premium because care is needed now. They are based on how much income you will need and the insurance company's assessment of how long you are likely to need the annuity income.

You have to pay a lump sum to the insurance company and the amount required will depend on:

- The level of income required
- Your age & health
- Current annuity rates
- Your life expectancy

So the poorer your health and/or the lower your life expectancy the cheaper the premium will be!

For extra cost, variables can be built into the policy, such as:

- Future price increases in the cost of care
- Capital protection clauses can be incorporated which allows some of the lump sum payment to be repaid to your estate if you die earlier than expected
- A 'deferred' option – so you can defer when you take the income to a later date

You have to balance having a regular secure income to pay for care against losing a lump sum invested in the policy were you to die early. Once you have taken the immediate care plan out, you are not able to cancel the plan and obtain a repayment of the lump sum even if you no longer require care.

10.7 Checklist
- As part of reviewing your finances on say retirement, include consideration of how you might fund care if it is needed in the future – if you do not own your home the only considerations will be whether you are eligible for LA assistance; or whether

your state of health will justify NHS continuing care funding; or whether you will have to pay for it yourself.

- Where you are dependent on the LA to fund your care there may well be little choice of care home available for the fees which the LA will pay.
- You may not be entitled to any LA support because your savings and income are too high. You are more likely to be concerned with estate planning to mitigate IHT on death in which case Chapter 7 will be more appropriate. You may consider investing in a long-term care plan.
- To discuss end of life planning choose a regulated practitioner to provide you with advice as part of putting in place a Lasting Power of Attorney and a Will.
- If tax planning is not relevant because your total estate is below the Nil Rate Band (see Chapter 7) and you do own your home make sure you have thought about how you own that property and whether making a change would be helpful alongside reviewing your Will.
- Be wary of gifting your house to your children not just because you are anxious about it being taken into account for assessing entitlement to means-tested benefits but for the practical reasons that once given you may be unable to get it back or use its sale proceeds.
- There are specialist IFAs who can advise you on the costs of obtaining long term care plans – see https://societyoflaterlifeadvisers.co.uk.

Chapter 11: What you need to know about public bodies who may be able to help you

With the reduction in the availability of legal aid and the high cost of regulation in the regulated sector causing fees for legal advice to rise, it is increasingly difficult to find legal advice at an affordable price.

In this concise guide I do not seek to cover in detail the many bodies concerned with regulating activities in every field. A visit to your local **Citizen's Advice Bureau** may help ascertain whether your problem is a legal one and whether you will need to fund the legal advice yourself or whether you are eligible for financial assistance. They are likely to know which regulatory body relates to a concern you may have if you are not able to fund legal advice. To find your local office see https://www.citizensadvice.org.uk/about-us/how-we-provide-advice/advice/search-for-your-local-citizens-advice.

In the UK there are official regulators or supervisory authorities which cover a variety of activities, and these are a good place to start if you have a serious concern.

Some matters are best dealt with by direct action – such as a problem with the quality of a product sold to you in a shop, which may not justify bringing a small claim in the county court if you cannot get redress from the seller. It maybe that notifying the Trading Standards Department of your local council may enable your grievance to be investigated. A trading standards officer acts on behalf of consumers and businesses to advise on, and enforce, laws that govern the way goods and services are bought, sold and hired. To find your local office see https://www.gov.uk/find-local-trading-standards-office

You may not have enjoyed a meal you had at a restaurant, bar or take-away which made you ill or you were put off by the lack of cleanliness of the premises. You should contact the Environmental Health Office of your local council. Environmental Health Officers are responsible for carrying out measures for protecting public health, including administering and enforcing legislation related to environmental health and providing support to minimize health and safety hazards. http://adlib.everysite.co.uk/adlib/defra/content.aspx?id=000IL3890W.16NTBYC4N021T4.

Other examples include, Ofsted: the Office for Standards in Education, Children's Services and Skills. This is a non-ministerial department reporting to Parliament. Ofsted is responsible for inspecting a range of educational institutions, including state schools and some independent schools. It also inspects childcare, adoption and fostering agencies and initial teacher training, and regulates a range of early years and children's social care services. The Chief Inspector (HMCI) is appointed by an Order-in-Council and thus becomes an office holder under the Crown. Amanda Spielman has been HMCI since 2017. http://www.ofsted.gov.uk

If your concern relates to a charity, contact the Charity Commission for England and Wales which is the non-ministerial government department that regulates registered charities in England and Wales and maintains the Central Register of Charities. The Charity Commission answers directly to the UK Parliament rather than to Government ministers. It is governed by a board, which is assisted by the Chief Executive (currently Helen Stephenson CBE) and an executive team. It has four sites in London, Taunton, Liverpool and Newport. The commission's website lists the latest accounts submitted by charities in England and Wales. https://www.gov.uk/government/organisations/charity-commission.

Your concern may be a healthcare matter. Your legal adviser will probably have sought to resolve your problem locally with the NHS or private body concerned. If you feel the need to go further, the Parliamentary and Health Service Ombudsman is the official body which makes final decisions on complaints that have not been resolved by the NHS in England or by a UK government department or other public organisation. The Parliamentary and Health Service Ombudsman service is free.

If you are unhappy with the final response from your GP practice or the NHS in your region, you can refer your complaint to the Health Service Ombudsman. You must have received a final response to your complaint before the ombudsman can look at it. The ombudsman will need a copy of this in writing. There is good guidance on what to do at http://www.ombudsman.org. uk/.

There are a host of other bodies concerned with healthcare. You should discuss these with your legal adviser who may refer you to one of these. Each has its own website. The relevant bodies are:

- Care Quality Commission (CQC)
- NHS Improvement (NHSI)
- Complementary and Natural Healthcare Council (CNHC)
- General Chiropractic Council (GCC)
- General Dental Council (GDC)
- General Medical Council (GMC)
- General Optical Council (GOC)
- General Osteopathic Council (GOsC)
- General Pharmaceutical Council (GPhC)
- Health and Care Professions Council (HCPC)
- Health and Safety Executive
- Human Fertilisation and Embryology Authority
- Medicines and Healthcare products Regulatory Agency (MHRA)
- Nursing and Midwifery Council (NMC)
- Pharmaceutical Society of Northern Ireland (PSNI)
- Professional Standards Authority for Health and Social Care

The legal profession regulators might be able to help with complaints about members of their part of the legal profession. To see the list of regulators look in Chapter 14.

For Social care, see

- Care Council for Wales (CCW)
- General Social Care Council (GSCC)
- Northern Ireland Social Care Council (NISCC)
- Scottish Social Services Council (SSSC)

For Transport, see

- Civil Aviation Authority (CAA)
- Office of Rail and Road (ORR)

For Utilities, see

- Ofcom – independent regulator and competition authority for the UK communications industries
- Phone-paid Services Authority – regulator for phone-paid services in the UK, part of Ofcom, replaces ICSTIS, PhonepayPlus
- Office for Nuclear Regulation (ONR)
- Ofgem – the Office of the Gas and Electricity Markets
- Ofwat – the Water Services Regulation Authority
- The Utility Regulator – regulating electricity, gas, water and sewerage industries in Northern Ireland
- Water Industry Commissioner for Scotland

For other bodies, see

- Advertising Standards Authority (ASA)
- British Board of Film Classification (BBFC)
- Citizens Advice and Citizens Advice Scotland (formerly Consumer Focus) – the statutory consumer champions for England, Wales, and Scotland
- Competition and Markets Authority (CMA)
- Council for Registered Gas Installers
- Direct Marketing Authority
- Engineering Council – the regulatory body for the engineering profession
- Equality and Human Rights Commission (EHRC)
- Food Standards Agency
- Forensic Science Regulator
- Gambling Commission [1]
- Gaming Board for Great Britain (GBGB)
- Gangmasters Licensing Authority
- IMPRESS
- Independent Press Standards Organisation (IPSO)
- Information Commissioner's Office
- Oil and Gas Authority (OGA)
- Planning Inspectorate
- Independent Police Complaints Commission
- Scottish Housing Regulator (SHC)
- Security Industry Authority

Chapter 12: How is law made?

12.1.1 Introduction

The law and legal systems of Scotland and, to a lesser extent, Northern Ireland, are distinct from those of England and Wales. Essentially, the law of England is the law of England and Wales, although devolution is making for differences in Wales too.

Whilst the law in Scotland and Northern Ireland will frequently coincide with that of the rest of the country don't assume that this is always the case. For example, the criminal law system is organised differently in Scotland and, in Northern Ireland, they do not have Lasting Powers of Attorney.

The reason for the difference is history. The jurisdictions have evolved over time. Until 2016 all parts of the UK had the same tax laws but even this is changing with the granting of taxing powers as part of the devolutionary process.

12.1.2 Statute or Acts of Parliament

A statute or Act is made by parliament. The intended Act has to pass through 'readings' in each House of Parliament (both the House of Commons and the House of Lords). To finally become law, it has to receive the agreement of the Queen.

An Act may be passed to address an immediate need or it can be part of a planned process to introduce a comprehensive code set out in the sections and schedules of an Act. It is not uncommon for an Act of Parliament to also be used to change existing law that has been decided by the courts if the government of the day believes the wrong decision has been made. A frequent example of this is the use of the annual Finance Act by Her Majesty's Revenue & Customs (HMRC) to 'correct' decisions made by the Courts with which it disagrees.

12.1.3 Subordinate Legislation

This is legislation that is introduced by regulations. The power to introduce subordinate legislation is granted to a government minister or local authority or public corporation.

Parliament when deciding upon an Act may grant authority to a government department or statutory authority to introduce subordinate legislation to fill in the details of the framework that the Act itself introduced. A good example of this is the Care Act 2014. It is merely a framework and below it is a raft of 22 regulations which flesh out the details.

Subordinate legislation is normally introduced by **statutory instrument** and can be regulations, orders made by a Secretary of State or Minister or in the form of rules. A large part of our legislation is introduced through this method. This makes it difficult to establish when certain parts of Acts of Parliament have actually started to apply. It also makes finding out the detailed rules difficult for the inexperienced.

Because subordinate legislation does not have to pass through Parliament it is changeable and can sometimes be amended several times, for example, the National Assistance (Assessment of Resources Regulations) 1992 was amended three times in 1993 once in 1994 twice in 1995 and once in 1996.

12.1.4 Common Law

Decided cases in the courts are part of what is known as 'the common law'. It was based originally on the common customs of the country and unwritten. Today, it is often described as 'judge made law' because it is the law as developed through decisions of judges in specific cases.

The courts can develop the common law only on a case-by-case basis. It is both remarkably flexible and at times frustrating. Flexible, because if the right cases come before the court it can develop the law very rapidly and address needs which are otherwise not covered by legislation. For example, the only authorities in the English legal system for the making of advance directives before the coming into force of the Mental Capacity Act 2005 were the principles enunciated in three leading cases involving patients in hospitals.

The common law is also frustrating because it may take a long while for the principle at issue to be fully established through a series of cases. If the problem is not one which the government of the day sees fit to improve or clarify by an Act of Parliament lawyers may have to interpret and apply the decisions from the cases to problems in everyday life.

In *Parker v British Airways Board* [1982] QB 1004 at p.1008 Lord Donaldson said that the judges

> *"have both the right and duty to extend and adapt the common law in the light of established principles and the current needs of the community. This is not to say that we start with a clean sheet. In doing so we should draw from the experience of the past as revealed by the previous decisions of the court."*

For those who wish to explore the influence which individual judges have had over the development of the common law you need look no further than any judgement of Lord Denning when sitting in the Court of Appeal and *The Politics of the Judiciary* by Griffiths.

The expression *common law* also includes the so-called rules of *equity*. These rules were a separate body of rules which ran alongside the *common law* until the two were amalgamated in the 19th Century to form the Supreme Court. The rules of *equity* were based on fairness.

12.1.5 Custom

As Lord Denning said in *The Secretary of State for Foreign and Common Wealth Affairs ex parte Indian Association of Alberta* [1982] QB 892 p.910:

> *"... they had their chiefs and head men to regulate their simple society and to enforce their customs. I say "to enforce their customs" because in early societies custom is the basis of law. Once a custom is established it gives rise to rights and obligations which the chiefs and head men will enforce. These customary laws are not written down. They are handed down by tradition from one generation to another. Yet beyond a doubt they are well established and have the force of law within the community."*

Our early common law was based on custom. In fact, the modern consumer law we have today has its roots back in the customs of the early medieval fairs. Today custom pays virtually no part in the development of our law.

12.1.6 European Union

Since the UK became a member of the European Community on the 1st January 1973 the Treaty of Rome has had direct effect in the UK. European Community Law consists of various treaties, Acts of Accession, regulations, decisions, directives and rights, liabilities, obligations and restrictions that from time to time arise by or under the treaties. Treaties do not have immediate binding effect in UK law instead they have largely been brought into effect by statute e.g. the UK Human Rights Act 1998 brought into effect the EU Convention on Human Rights.

Regulations and decisions in the European Union have been immediately binding on coming into force. Directives are addressed to member states that are required to bring in appropriate legislation within a specific timescale. For example, the 4th EU Anti Money Laundering Directive was agreed in 2015 and had to come into effect in the UK by June 2017.

Disputes over legislation or subordinate legislation by the European Union must be decided upon not by English judges but by the European Court of Justice which does not operate in the same way as the courts in England in that each case is decided on its merit rather than on the basis of prior decisions.

The supremacy of European Union law was recognised by the House of Lords in *R v Darby* [1980] 2 ALL ER 166. In the time since then some have resented the impact this has had on UK law, which was one of the factors that resulted in the referendum decision in June 2016 to leave the EU.

For now, until the UK leaves the EU, the UK courts are under a duty to give a purposive construction to regulations in such a manner as would accord with the decisions of the European Court of Justice. Where points of EU law arise the courts in the UK must refer these points to the European Court of Justice for a decision before coming to a conclusion in the matter.

12.1.7 Court structure

It is fundamental to the way the English legal system operates that the lower courts are bound by decisions reached by the higher courts. This is the system of precedent which aims to avoid uncertainty.

The effect of the system of precedent is that the main decisions of a higher court must be applied by a lower court in any similar case unless and until is it overruled by a higher court or by Act of Parliament.

The Supreme Court

Decisions of the Supreme Court (formerly known as the House of Lords) are binding on all lower courts.

The main problem in relation to the Supreme Court (and it predecessors) has always been whether it should be bound by its own previous decisions. In 1966 the House of Lords stated that rigid adherence to the principle of precedent might lead to injustice in some cases and unduly restrict the development of the law and that the House should be able to depart from its own decisions where it appears right to do so. Sparing use has been made of this power.

The Court of Appeal

It is **bound** by the decisions of the **Supreme Court**. Its decisions bind all lower courts.

In **civil** cases, it is **bound by its own previous decisions** unless one of the following exceptions applies:

(i) The court may choose between two conflicting decisions of its own – the case which is not applied is deemed to be **overruled**;
(ii) The court must not follow its own decision if that is inconsistent with a later decision of the Supreme Court; and
(iii) Where the court is satisfied that the earlier decision was made without due care – i.e. the decision was made without reference to all relevant cases and statutes of authority.

In **criminal** cases, it is bound by its own decisions with the same exceptions as above but with one additional exception – that it may override a previous decision on the basis that the law has been misapplied or misunderstood and it is necessary to overrule the decision in the interests of justice – an exception which has been frequently invoked in recent years.

The Court of Appeal may **overrule** decisions of the lower courts.

The High Court

The High Court is bound by the decisions of the Supreme Court and the Court of Appeal unless made without due care. The High Court comprises:

The Divisional Court (where two or more judges sit) this court is bound by its own previous decisions unless one of the exceptions apply.

The judge sitting at the first instance: when a single judge considers a case for the first time he is bound by the decisions of the Supreme Court and the Court of Appeal and the Divisional Court (i.e. of two or more high court judges sitting alone).

A single judge is not bound by the decisions made by another High Court judge sitting alone. However, a High Court judge will naturally treat previous decisions of the court as persuasive and will only refuse to follow them if he is convinced that they are wrong.

Inferior courts

The County Court, Crown Court and Magistrates' Courts are inferior courts. They are bound by decisions in the higher courts but their own decisions are not binding. They do not form binding precedent mainly because they are not reported and so would be impossible to find.

Certain Special Courts and Tribunals

There are a large number of different courts and tribunals created to deal with matters arising under modern legislation for example employment cases for unfair dismissal or redundancy are heard in **industrial tribunals** and the **Employment Appeals Tribunal** hears appeals from tribunals on points of law.

Another special tribunal is the **Probate Registry**. There are 30 local probate registries in England and Wales; two in Scotland and one in Northern Ireland. These registries are run under a Probate Registrar who is equivalent in status to a Deputy Judge in the County Court.

The Principal Probate Registry is located in London and the senior probate registrar reports to the President of the Family Division of the High Court. This is the Court responsible for the certification process confirming the validity of the Will or confirmation of the appointment of Administrators in an intestacy.

The work of the Probate Registrar is non-contentious. It is governed by the Non-Contentious Probate Rules 1987 as amended. These rules cover all sorts of issues like the procedure for issuing grants to an attorney and the type of evidence required to show the Will was properly executed.

The European Court of Justice

The European Court of Justice operates under the treaties of the European community. The court consists of judges appointed from each of the member states, and they are assisted by Advocates – General, a type of official unknown to the English legal system. It is his task to present the court with a summary of the law as he judges it to be. Usually, the court will accept the Advocate General's submissions, but it need not do so.

The jurisdiction of the court may be subdivided as follows:

(a) Matters concerning the conduct of member states or of community institutions, such as hearing complaints brought by the Commission that a member state has failed to fulfil its obligations, for example by not implementing a directive.
(b) Actions for compensation for wrongful damage caused by the community institutions or their servants in the course of their duties.
(c) Disputes between the communities and their servants.
(d) Matters of direct concern to litigants or prospective litigants in England. This covers the preliminary rulings mentioned earlier on the interpretation of treaties etc. Where such a question is raised before a court in England that court may (or the in the case of a matter before the Supreme Court, it must) refer the matter to the European Court of Justice for a ruling. Once made it is then the responsibility of the local courts to apply that law as thus interpreted.

12.2 Why is the law different in different places?

Different legal traditions have arisen through history. English law carried its principles across the Empire and many countries in the Commonwealth have a basis in English law even if they have developed their own traditions since independence e.g. India. Within a country there may be separate jurisdictions e.g. the USA because it is a federal country with different states; Switzerland with its 26 federal cantons in its Confederation.

In England, the theory of law used is based on the common law but in most of the EU states the tradition is quite different. It is based on a civil code – a kind of contract between the state and the citizen. Wherever Napoleon succeeded across the battlefields of Europe in the 18th and 19th Centuries so he took the French system of the civil code with him. This has resulted in a very different set of traditions.

Common Law Country e.g. England	Civil Law Country e.g. France or Spain
No matrimonial property regime	Matrimonial Property Regime e.g. in France everything is owned jointly and severally in a communal pot both parties to the marriage being jointly and severally liable for debts. Unless, the parties enter into a contract that separates each person's property so that each has control over their own property whenever they acquired it and they each remain solely liable for their personal debts or there is a joint participation in the goods acquired only during the marriage.
Testamentary freedom – the ability to leave your estate to who you want.	Forced heirship – particular people are automatically entitled to a portion of your estate, whether you want them to benefit or not.

Discretionary power of the Court, e.g. Inheritance (Provision for Family and Dependants) Act 1975 to adjust the results of testamentary freedom.	No similar discretionary powers.
On death your property belongs to your PRs. The beneficiaries merely have a right to their inheritance. The PRs are liable to the deceased's creditors only up to the value of the assets in the estate.	Assets and Liabilities belong to the forced heirs directly if they accept the inheritance.
Domicile – your permanent home – is what connects you to the laws of succession and jurisdiction of the courts.	Habitual residence or nationality – is what connects you to the laws of succession and jurisdiction of the courts.
Trusts – are part of our legal system.	No trusts are recognised.

These differences are what make life difficult for the global citizen with assets located in more than one jurisdiction. There is no mechanism for making the different legal systems work in harmony which makes for uncertainty and expense; although within the EU there is the Succession Regulation 650/2012, designed to enable choices to be made to have one set of succession laws apply to your whole estate wherever it is located within the EU.

12.3 Where to find the law
12.3.1 Law reports
The system of precedent described above depends on a good system of law reports. These publications contain the more important decisions given by the courts and tribunals.

Although law reporting as such has been in existence since at least the 13th century it was not a formalised system until the late 19th century when in 1875 the Incorporated Council of Law Reporting for England and Wales started publishing an official series of reports under the title **The Law Reports**.

The reports are an annual bound set of separate volumes for each division of the High Court and the Court of Appeal and the Supreme Court. These law reports have priority in court because the judge who heard the case sees and revises the report before it is published.

In 1953, the Council began to publish the reports weekly in what is known as **The Weekly Law Reports**. This series includes not only the decisions that will appear in subsequent additions of **The Law Reports** but also decisions that justify publication because they are of interest.

There are in addition those private publications of case reports of which the most comprehensive and best known is the **All England Law Reports**. By subscription these may now be searched over the Internet.

To enable free access to law reports an organisation has established a reporting system and this is a good source of case law for everyone, lawyers and non-lawyers alike. It is called the British and Irish Legal Information Institute or Bailii for short. It provides access to freely available British and Irish Public Legal Information and can be found at http://www.bailii.org.

Whichever law reporting system one subscribes to there is a voluminous amount of paper issued each year. Increasingly researchers use the worldwide web where the main publishers can offer their services over the Internet.

To look up cases you ideally need the name of both the parties, and the citation (i.e. a reference to the law report series where your case can be found in a coded form) or the parties and the year. Modern law reports date from 1865 onwards and where the date is certain square brackets are used for example *Donoghue v Stephenson* [1932] AC 562.

New specialist case law services have developed over time for example the **Wills & Trusts Law Reports**, was launched in 2000 by Legalease under the auspices of the Society of Trust and Estate

Practitioners (STEP). This publication just publishes cases relevant to the Trust and Estate practitioner.

12.3.2 How do you find a statute and whether it is in effect?

Acts of Parliament are published by H.M.S.O once they have reached the statute book. These can now be viewed on the web and hard copies ordered if necessary from http://www.hmso.gov. uk. There is also a free online archive to be found at http://www. legislation.gov.uk.

It is also possible to follow progress of bills through the parliamentary site at http://www.parliament.uk.

Each statute is numbered sequentially throughout the year; this is the chapter number. For example, the Trusts of Land and an Appointment of Trustees Act 1996 is chapter 47 in that year.

Whilst statutes come into force on the given date it is important to check whether a statute, either in whole or in part is in force at any given time. A classic example of an Act that came in, in stages over several years was the Children's Act 1989. For this you need some kind of system. The one commonly used in practice is **'Is it in force?'** which is in an annual paper backed volume, part of the Halsbury's Statutes. It is a guide to the commencement of the statutes of England and Wales and of Scotland passed since 1st January. Most law firms will also subscribe to Halsbury's Laws, which consists of over 50 volumes, indexes and supplements describing the current law on each subject area. This work is often in major reference libraries.

Use this tool when you want to search:

(i) Subject area – views Halsbury's Laws Consolidated Index
(ii) Specific pieces of legislation – use the Halsbury's Laws consolidated table of statutes
(iii) A case – start by using Halsbury's Laws Consolidated table of Cases

From any of these three sources you will get a reference to a volume and paragraph in the main text volumes. Then bring the main volumes up to date by using the same references for volume and paragraph in the cumulative supplements addition. There is even a current service noter-up, which is in the form of a loose-leaf binder and again there are sections where you would look up the relevant volume, title and paragraph to see if there had been any further changes.

Another common publication used to find information is the Current Law Service, which again takes the form of a legislation citator and case citator.

12.3.3 Other sources

The use of legal portals can be one way of accessing changes in all areas of law and finding information and commentaries prepared by law firms or barristers. The leading legal portal is one maintained by Delia Venables, which can be found at http:// www.venables.co.uk.

As a consequence of the volume of sources of law there are many commentaries on the law such as encyclopaedias, digests, textbooks, journals, dictionaries etc. These are known as secondary sources, the primary sources being the original written statutes and cases.

Textbooks are very useful in explaining the subject area and largely they are aimed at either students or the practitioner. Practitioners' textbooks tend to be large and costly bound volumes. It can therefore be an expensive business always having the latest edition of the textbook that is of course essential to keep up to date with the changes in the law. For this reason, many publishers produce textbooks in either loose-leaf form for practitioners who have subscribed or more frequently publishers provide a subscription service online which has the advantage that access to the data is by use of a computer search. It also enables precedents to be used on screen without having to type in the document.

Journals are also a useful way of keeping up to date and reading specific titles relevant to an area of expertise is useful such as **Taxation; Law Society's Gazette; The New Law Journal; Private Client Business; Trusts and Estates etc**.

12.4 Checklist

12.4.1 Do you have any knowledge at all?

The first place to look might be a relevant text book -

For example, if we wanted to know the sources of law for Advance Decisions we would see in the Index of Elderly Clients – A Precedent Manual (5ᵗʰ Edition) 2016 *Jordans,* by Caroline Bielanska that under the index Chapter 12 is dedicated to this topic. Here reference is made to statute, case law and the history. This gives a good starting point to the main sources of law:

Primary source: Mental Capacity Act 2005

Secondary sources: Case law – in particular Re T (Adult: refusal of treatment) [1992] 4 All ER 649; Mental Capacity Act 2005 Code of Practice, para 9.37

12.4.2 If you have no knowledge about an area
The prime starting point for discussion of a subject is Halsbury's Laws. The index again would need to be searched and in the commentary, check out the references to statute and case law. Halsbury's Laws is such a huge resource it is only completely updated many years apart so in between there is the cumulative supplement – every time a new supplement is issued it replaces the earlier ones; and the noter-up service which is loose-leaf to bring everything almost bang up to date. The cumulative supplement and the noter-up service use the same volume, paragraph and page numbers as the main service so that you can link up easily.

12.4.3 If you are looking to see if a statute has been updated
When you have identified the relevant prime legislation, it is necessary to check whether it is still in force or if it has been modified in any way or indeed whether parts of the Act are not yet in force. To do this the Halsbury service "Is it in force?" is a check or the equivalent Current Law Statutes service can advise.

12.4.4 If you are looking to see if a case is still current law
When you have the main prime sources of law it may be that there has been judicial consideration given to the interpretation of a particular part of the legislation or case law which has developed the common law.

A check would therefore have to be made of the Current Law Yearbook, or the monthly digest to bring yourself right up to date. This service not only gives you a thumbnail sketch of the case in the yearbook or monthly digest it will also give you the other references for where the full text of the case is reported and reference to other books or articles published in the particular area of law.

Chapter 13: Where lawyers fit into the English legal system

There are several different types of lawyer and not all of them are regulated (see Chapter 14). Each type of lawyer has a prime purpose and some have more than one which can make it difficult to know which is right for you.

13.1 Where do lawyers fit into the English legal system?

Lawyers are people who uphold the rule of law in a democracy. The concept of the rule of law means that everyone is equal before the law and its application is enforced by judges who are independent of the executive and Parliament.

A recent example of upholding the rule of law was when an ordinary citizen challenged the action of the Government through the courts over the triggering of Article 50 to start the exit of the UK from the EU. The Government had to put its arguments as to how this was to be done to the Courts – eventually the Supreme Court – which, through the Judges of the Supreme Court, resolved whether the actions were lawful or not. The claimant won and the Government had to put the triggering of Article 50 to a vote in the Houses of Parliament rather than just trigger the process when it chose using executive powers.

Lawyers seek justice for others, which means helping to find the truth, a bit like an investigative journalist would do, and then use the law to seek redress for the person in need. This includes, for example, obtaining compensation for an injured person; or helping someone to avoid deportation or defending a person against prosecution on a criminal charge.

Some of these areas used to be covered by Legal Aid, a financially means tested system to ensure anyone could pursue a justifiable claim or defence even if they did not have enough money themselves to fund the course of action. After 30 years, the Legal Aid system has been systematically undermined and is now far from freely available. The bodies representing legal professionals have challenged government over their commitment to Legal Aid, there have been Court boycotts and marches but sadly to no avail so that there are some parts of England which are Legal Aid deserts – that is, no-one authorised or willing to undertake work funded by Legal Aid. Also, some areas of practice are no longer funded by Legal Aid, such as divorce.

Lawyers do not only act for individuals but also businesses of all kinds, governments, charities, trusts and other legal entities. Their collective skill is to ascertain whether their client has a legal problem and if so how it should be addressed. It might be by negotiation or mediation rather than through the court system.

Lawyers also perform legal services which are not necessarily contentious but are part of a process of ensuring the correct legal outcome. For example, transferring the legal ownership of a property to its new rightful owner – this could include investigating whether the legal title to a property is correct; checking the planning consent is appropriate for the client's preferred use of the land & buildings; ensuring the use the client wants it for will be possible e.g. it is correctly connected to services and roads; dealing with the provider(s) of any funds to purchase the property and putting in place appropriate ancillary documents such as declarations as to who has contributed what to the purchase price and the terms on which they expect to be repaid or have an interest in the property; paying the correct amount of tax on the transaction (Stamp Duty Land Tax in England) and attending to the registration of the transaction at the Land Registry.

Whilst it is not compulsory to use a lawyer, it is nearly always advantageous as they will be familiar with the law and have experience of appearing in a particular court or tribunal, in the case of a barrister or those solicitors able to appear in the particular court or tribunal.

However, either from necessity or choice, more and more people are seeking to act for themselves. Although it is said a person who acts for him or herself has a fool for a client, this is not entirely true. There is helpful information on many areas within the www. gov.uk website; there are places on the web to obtain the details of the law for free and some websites provide information and support by the production of forms and guidance notes to take matters forward. Nevertheless, caution should be the DIY lawyer's watchword. Free websites may not be accurate or accept any liability for the accuracy of their content. Also, the DIY lawyer may be up against skilled lawyers familiar with both the law and the processes and procedures placing the novice at a disadvantage.

13.2 The different types of lawyer operating in England

Just as trees are but one species that populates a wood so lawyers are just one type of person who offer legal services, study the law or administer the law. Lawyers are the generic name for all those who study, practice and adjudicate the law. If you like, lawyers are like the different varieties of tree in the wood; there are other people and organisations offering some legal services who are not lawyers, just as there are other species in a wood which are not trees, like bracken and lichen.

The common types of lawyers that you may meet or need in practice are:

*   **Judges** are specially selected lawyers who administer justice from the inferior courts to the Supreme Court. Senior Judges are law lords and have a distinguished background of practice in the law before being made a Senior Judge. They are responsible for hearing cases put to them by claimants or prosecutors and deciding on the outcome by reference to the law.
*   **Barristers** practice as independent lawyers in what are known as 'chambers' or 'sets'. These groupings allow for sharing of overheads such as paying the rent on rooms and library costs. Some barristers may be academics or no longer practice but carry out a legal role within a business. To practice as a barrister a person has to be insured and comply with the requirements of their regulator – the Bar Standards Board.

Barristers are known for their advocacy skills – that is, the ability to argue a case before a court or tribunal on behalf of a client. While this is a special skill they are no longer unique in being able to perform it. Those offering legal services who have a 'right of audience' can also appear before a court or tribunal on behalf of someone else.

In addition to advocacy, barristers also research the law and provide expert opinions on it to other lawyers, tax experts and in some cases directly to the public.

In 2015 there were 15,899 practising barristers in England and Wales and 409 sets of chambers https://www.barstandardsboard. org.uk/media-centre/research-and-statistics/statistics/chambers.

Members of the public can access a barrister directly now through the Public Access scheme. Previously, access to a member of the Bar was only via a solicitor who put the legal case to the barrister for an opinion or instructed the barrister to appear in court. To take part in the public access scheme a barrister has to undertake special training. You can find out what a barrister can do for you and how to find one suitably qualified by looking at this website:

http://www.barcouncil.org.uk/media/119600/public_access_ guidance_for_lay_clients_-_mar_2010_-_as_at_25_oct_2011__1_. pdf

• **Solicitors** can practice in sole practice; as part of a firm; in-house for businesses or local or national government and in the military. Solicitors too can be academics and may no longer practice. Firms can be organised as general partnerships, limited liability partnerships or as limited companies. Solicitors can also be part of an Alternative Business Structure – a relatively new structure which permits non-lawyers to invest in legal services alongside lawyers.

To practice, a solicitor has to be insured and comply with the requirements of their regulator – the Solicitors Regulation Authority (SRA). Some solicitors appear in court. No specialist advocacy requirement is needed to appear in the Magistrate's Court or the County Court and some Tribunals but where 'higher rights of audience' are exercised in e.g. the High Court and above, then the solicitor has to have an advocacy qualification.

Most solicitor's work involves seeing clients on whose behalf legal work is undertaken which may involve researching the law or carrying out a legal process such as making their Will. Some work involves collecting evidence and preparing a case to send to a Barrister to present in court. All kinds of different work is undertaken by solicitors from Aviation law to Will preparation and everything in between. As the law is complex, most solicitors specialise in one or two connected areas, such as Wills & Probate; Company & Commercial law; or, Property taxes & Land Law.

Solicitors with a practising certificate are authorised to perform reserved legal activities (see Chapter 14).

In December 2016 there were 135,309 practising solicitors in England and Wales (http://www.sra.org.uk/sra/how-we-work/reports/data/population_solicitors.page) of which 54,924 work in the top 100 (by size) law firms http://www.lawsociety.org.uk/support-services/research-trends/research-roundup-winter-2016.

- **Alternative Business Structures** – since the coming into force of the Legal Services Act 2007 it is possible for other businesses to offer legal services not just law firms and barristers. Alternative Business Structures (or ABSs) are simply a vehicle which permits people other than lawyers to invest in organisations which provide legal and other services, in some case, regulated legal activities. Despite its name, the Solicitors Regulation Authority regulates ABSs – http://www.sra.org.uk/sra/equality-diversity/impact-assessments/alternative-business-structures.page.

The purpose behind the introduction of ABSs was to provide you the consumer with more choice of providers and permit multi-disciplinary practices to form so you could find a 'one-stop shop' for a bundle of services which otherwise you would have to purchase from a range of separate providers. Perhaps the most well-known ABS is the Co-op which provides certain legal services such as Will drafting, estate administration and divorce as well as providing funeral services.

The practical outcome of using an ABS rather than any old business or company is that it too is regulated in much the same way as a firm of solicitors and by the same regulator.

- **Members of the Chartered Institute of Legal Executives** (CILex) are people who can practice in law firms either as part of a multi-faceted partnership where they can be employed or where they can be a partner or in practices of their own. For many years, members of CILex have worked in law firms with solicitors, supporting solicitors in their work or working alongside them. There are distinct groups of CILex membership:

- o Fellows, Legal Accounts Executives, Graduate members, Legal Accounts Members, Associate members and Associate Prosecutors
- o Individuals with practice rights in probate and conveyancing who are not members of CILex but are nevertheless regulated by CILex Regulation
- o Student members, Affiliate members, Non-Practising members

Since 2013 CILEx members are able to set up as a sole practitioner, in a partnership, as a company or charity. Sole practitioner CILEx members cannot provide reserved legal activities (see Chapter 14). However, sole practitioner Fellows can provide the reserved legal activity of administering oaths – that is, witnessing the signing of papers on oath which are needed for use in Court or in a legal process.

CILex members can study for their qualifications while working rather than having to do a degree first or qualifying legal practice course, each of which are costly on fees. In fact, this route provides an alternative means of entering the solicitors' profession as a Fellow can take the legal practice course in order to qualify as a solicitor if they wish.

- • **Paralegals** are a relatively new addition to the field. Sadly, as a result of the reduction in the availability of training contracts to become a barrister or solicitor, graduates have sought legal positions in an effort to use their legal knowledge and hopefully be given the opportunity of a training contract at some point. Paralegals are often, but not exclusively, law graduates who could not afford to pursue the legal practice course or graduates of both who could not find a training contract.

The larger law firms seek paralegals to undertake high volume work or work which needs low cost personnel to undertake it. This is no criticism as many paralegals develop strong skills through internal training and development provided by their employer to progress to CILex membership or qualify as a solicitor in due course.

The National Association of Licensed Paralegals (NALP) is a self-regulatory body for its members and as such offers its members the opportunity to apply for a NALP Licence to Practise. It is recognised by Ofqual as a Qualifications Awarding Organisation. For more information see http://www.nationalparalegals.co.uk.

- **Apprenticeships** are paid jobs that incorporate on and off the job training. A successful apprentice will qualify with a nationally recognised qualification on completion of their contract. Over 2.4 million apprenticeships were started between 2010/11 and 2014/15. Although modern apprenticeships started before then there was an increase in the number of people starting an apprenticeship in 2015. More than half (54%) of all apprenticeship starts in 2015/16 were in two sectors: Business, Administration & Law and Health, Public Service & Care. (Source: House of Commons Briefing paper – Apprenticeship Statistics England by James Mirza-Davies, November 2016). See https://www.gov.uk/guidance/legal-services-apprenticeships.

In March 2013, degree level apprenticeships in legal services were launched – Higher Apprenticeship in Legal Service. The apprenticeship does not mean the apprentice qualifies as a solicitor or barrister at the end of the contract; rather it is designed as a pathway for the paralegal or qualified "fee earner" career route. See http://www.law.ac.uk/apprenticeships.

There is a school leaver one too – CILEx has developed a Trailblazer Paralegal Apprenticeship, which launched in September 2016. It is designed to help school leavers enter administrative work in the legal sector and to be a stepping stone for the Higher Apprenticeship in Legal Service. For more information see http://www.cilexlawschool.ac.uk/Trailblazer_Paralegal_Apprenticeship.

Slowly law firms are offering these apprenticeship contracts. There is government funding (with conditions) for employers offering these contracts.

- **Notaries** – According to the Notaries Society:

"A Notary is a qualified lawyer – a member of the third and oldest branch of the legal profession in England and Wales. Notaries are appointed by the Court of Faculties of the Archbishop of Canterbury and are subject to regulation by

171

the Master of the Faculties. The rules which affect Notaries are very similar to the rules which affect Solicitors. They must be fully insured and maintain fidelity cover for the protection of their clients and the public. They must keep clients' money separately from their own and comply with stringent practice rules and rules relating to conduct and discipline. Notaries have to renew their practising certificates every year and can only do so if they have complied with the rules."

Notaries are mostly concerned with the authentication and certification of signatures, authority and capacity relating to documents for use abroad.

They are also authorised to conduct general legal practice (excluding the conduct of court proceedings) such as conveyancing and probate. They may exercise the powers of a Commissioner for Oaths.

*   **Licensed Conveyancers** – the role of licensed conveyancer is relatively recent. In 1987 Parliament decided to open up the market and permit people other than solicitors to deal with property work. A licensed conveyancer is a lawyer who specialises in property work in England & Wales. They deal with the paperwork needed to finance a purchase and handle sale and purchase transactions. The Council for Licensed Conveyancers regulates members of this profession. Solicitors and legal executives can also carry out property work but are not limited to only undertake property work; whereas, property work is all that a licensed conveyancer is regulated to conduct.
*   **Licensed Probate Practitioners** – continuing the trend for people other than solicitors being permitted to conduct legal work, Parliament also authorised licensed probate practitioners to conduct the administration of estates. Again, solicitors, ABSs and legal executives can also still conduct this work but some people are licensed to only do probate work. Some licensed conveyancers are also licensed probate practitioners. Accountants can also apply for a licence to conduct probate work as their regulator, the Institute of Chartered Accountants of England & Wales, is approved to regulate and oversee members under the Legal Services Act 2007 (see Chapter 14) and more recently The Association of Chartered Certified Accountants (ACCA).

- **Trade Mark or Patent attorneys** – this is another highly specialised area of practice – the protection of an invention or novel idea or creative work by registering a patent requires the skills of someone who both understands what you have created and can advise on what can be protected and how to go about it. They can protect your designs, your creative work and brand names – your 'intellectual property'. These specialist attorneys may also help with the promotion of your ideas through producing licensing agreements and other legal documents. Trade Mark and Patent Attorneys are regulated by the Intellectual Property Regulation Board.

- **Costs Lawyers** – legal costs can be complicated to work out particularly in court cases because of rules which apply to the quantification and allocation of who pays these bills – the winner, the loser, the estate – in particular circumstances. As court cases and other transactions can last for long periods of time and permitted rates of charging may have varied over time a Costs Lawyer can provide specialist advice on actual bills and billing in general to costs management and costs budgeting. The Costs Lawyers Standards Board is also known as the CLSB, and is responsible for regulating Costs Lawyers with a practising certificate working in England and Wales.

- **Unregulated lawyers** – not all people providing legal services are regulated. There are some lawyers who are not regulated who are able to provide certain legal services which include:
  - **Will writers** – Will writing is not a regulated legal service so anyone can offer to prepare your Will, whether or not they are properly trained and without being regulated or insured.
  - **McKenzie Friends** – These are people who are prepared to assist you in court – give you moral support if you are representing yourself and take notes and give you guidance. They are not able to act as your agent or speak in court on your behalf. Some of them charge for their services. Again, there is no particular qualification – they could simply be your friend or a member of the family.
  - **Charities & Trade Unions** – both types of body offer assistance with legal matters connected with their interests and those of their members. Some of the officers of the charity or Trade Union may be a regulated lawyer but this is not necessarily the case and they may be using volunteers to help you e.g. Citizen's Advice Bureau.

o **Mediators** – can help you when faced with a dispute which you want to resolve outside of going to court. There is no specific qualification required to be a mediator – anyone can call themselves a mediator. It is now the case that you must see a mediator before going to the Family law courts. Some may have professional qualifications but many do not.

The more that the legal market is opened up to try and make those offering legal services more competitive and so reduce the cost for consumers, the greater the confusion for consumers in knowing who is offering to work for them and whether they are trained, insured and regulated.

It is always worthwhile investigating whether the person offering to undertake work for you is regulated or not before deciding to instruct them to act for you.

13.3 Where to find the type of lawyer you need

As a consumer it is not easy to decide who to trust with your problem or transaction. Choosing the right type of lawyer may sadly depend on how much money you have available too. When you are not even sure whether your problem is a legal one or where you have multiple issues which need to be addressed, such as divorce and as a result you need someone to handle the sale of your property as well and make a Will for you; then it is probably best to go to a solicitor's firm offering a comprehensive range of services. If you simply want someone to handle your house move you could choose a Licensed Conveyancer or Legal Executive or a solicitor.

To make matters even more confusing, within the solicitor's profession there are a range of specialist services some of which have developed into separate professional bodies or accredited services. For example, if you have had an accident and are seeking compensation you might wish to see a solicitor who is a member of the Association of Personal Injury Lawyers. If you have a farm and wish to seek advice about your agricultural tenancy you might want someone who is a member of the Agricultural Law Association. If you want help with ensuring your family's succession to your estate is secure and any trusts properly managed then you should look for a member of the Society of Trusts and Estates Practitioners

(incidentally, this organisation has not only lawyers as members but other professionals who specialise in trust and estate advice such as accountants, bankers, IFA etc)

Solicitors who are members of specialist bodies or have gained accreditation in a particular area of practice will often make this clear on their headed notepaper and in their firm's literature.

Each type of regulated lawyer mentioned above offers a service to find a local member and the easiest way to utilise these services is via the website set up by the regulators: http://www.legalchoices. org.uk/legal-choices.

The Competition and Markets Authority conducted research into the ease with which consumers can find an appropriate lawyer and published their findings in December 2016 – https://www.gov.uk/government/publications/legal-services-cma-recommendations.

This book is concerned with the law and therefore lawyers operating in England and Wales. To find out more about the regulation of lawyers in Scotland see the website of the Law Society of Scotland – https://www.lawscot.org.uk and for the Advocates in Scotland (barristers in England) see http://www.advocates.org.uk.

To find out more about the regulation of lawyers in Northern Ireland see the website of the Law Society of Northern Ireland – https://www.lawsoc-ni.org and for barristers see the website of the Bar of Northern Ireland – http://www.barofni.com/page/regulation.

Chapter 14: The Regulatory Framework

14.1 Background

In 2004 Sir David Clementi presented his final report on his Review of the Regulatory Framework for Legal Services in England and Wales. The Legal Services Act 2007 was the result of his work. This Act confirms the list and scope of reserved activities for which the provider must be regulated and creates the framework for regulation of legal services. It created the oversight regulator (The Legal Services Board or LSB) which authorises regulatory bodies for each of the different types of regulated lawyers of which there are eight (see Chapter 13), the main ones being:

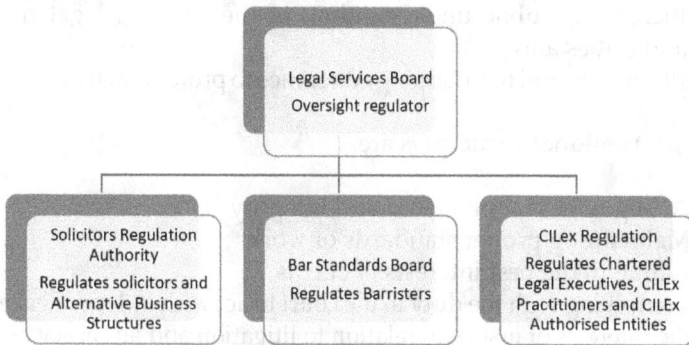

As Sir David pointed out in his final report:

"The definition of reserved legal services is relatively straightforward since those areas are contained in statute.... These areas could be termed the inner circle of legal services. In order to provide such services, a practitioner must be certified by a regulatory body which has itself been authorised to do so. A 'lawyer' could therefore be defined as any duly certified member of such a body."

14.2 Legal Services Board

The Legal Services Board (LSB) has been in operation since 1 January 2009 and regulates all the regulatory bodies and delegates day-to-day oversight of their members to the relevant regulatory body, reserving oversight only to itself.

The Legal Services Act 2007 established a comprehensive Ombudsman Scheme for the handling of complaints about regulated legal activities.

Under the Act the LSB is charged to promote and maintain **regulatory objectives** relating to the provision of legal services, namely:

1. Protecting and promoting public interest
2. Supporting the constitutional principle of the rule of law
3. Improving access to justice
4. Protecting and promoting the interests of consumers
5. Promoting competition in the provision of legal services
6. Encouraging an independent, strong, diverse and effective legal profession
7. Increasing public understanding of the citizen's legal rights and duties and
8. Promoting and maintaining adherence to professional principles

The **professional principles** are:

- Acting with independence and integrity
- Maintaining proper standards of work
- Acting in the best interests of clients
- Complying with the duty to the court to act with independence in the interests of justice in relation to litigation and advocacy and
- Keeping the affairs of clients confidential

Under s.28 Legal Services Act 2007, approved regulators are under a statutory duty to act in a way which is compatible with the regulatory objectives. Approved regulators must also have regard to the principles under which regulatory activities should be transparent, accountable, proportionate, consistent and targeted.

The Act has created a system whereby the providers of legal services have a choice of which of the approved regulators may regulate their firm. For example, a probate practitioner can choose to be regulated by the Solicitors Regulation Authority or by the Council for Licensed Conveyancers. From 31 March 2009, firms of solicitors only doing conveyancing and probate may choose to be regulated by the Council for Licensed Conveyancers in place of the

Solicitors Regulation Authority.

However, if a person remains as a solicitor, their firm might be regulated by the Council for Licensed Conveyancers but as an individual, the solicitor personally would remain regulated by the Solicitors Regulation Authority.

14.3 Regulated legal activities

Stephen Mayson on behalf of the Legal Services Institute wrote in 2010 that

> "Reserved legal activities are one of the fundamental building blocks of the Legal Services Act 2007. For example, they are pivotal to the definition of an 'authorised person' (section 18), to the designation of a regulator as an 'approved regulator' (section 20(5)), to the grant of licences to alternative business structures (section 11 (1)), and to the appointment of a Head of Legal Practice for an ABS (Schedule 11, paragraph 11(30)(b))."

Section 12 of the Legal Services Act 2007 first sets out the six specific legal services activities that only those who are authorised (or those who are exempt) can carry on. These are called "reserved legal activities" and their scope is set out in Schedule 2. The six areas are:

I. The exercise of a right of audience – which includes the right to appear before and address a court and examine witnesses.
II. The conduct of litigation – which includes the issuing, commencement, prosecution and defence of proceedings before any court in England and Wales, and the performance of any ancillary functions.
III. Reserved instrument activities – which includes the preparation of any instrument of transfer or charge for the purposes of Land Registration Act 2002 or ancillary documents relating to real or personal estate under the law of England and Wales; or other instruments relating to court proceedings in England and Wales.
IV. Probate activities – which includes preparing any probate papers for the purpose of the law of or in relation to any proceedings within England and Wales.
V. Notarial activities – includes activities which were customarily carried on by notaries in accordance with the Public Notaries Act 1801.
VI. The administration of oaths – which is the exercise of the

powers conferred on a commissioner for oaths by the Commissioners for Oaths Acts 1889 and 1891 and s.24 Stamp Duties Management Act 1891.

Certain people are exempt from being authorised even though they carry on the reserved activities e.g. a litigant in person, which is someone conducting his or her own legal work even though they are not a lawyer.

Equally, it is possible for probate activities to be carried out by an individual who is not authorised to do the work but who carries it on under the direction and supervision of an employer, manager or colleague who is an authorised person e.g. a paralegal working in a solicitors' firm; or who carries on the activities without being paid e.g. Citizen's Advice Bureau or a charity.

The regulatory framework is made more complex because the Legal Services Act 2007 regulates some legal activities which are not 'reserved legal activities' within s.12. These other activities are either legal activities carried out by individuals who are regulated in all the services they offer (e.g. all legal activities conducted by solicitors or barristers who are each regulated by either the Solicitors Regulation Authority or the Bar Standards Board) or legal activities that are otherwise regulated by statute even though they are not reserved legal activities (e.g. immigration, claims management and insolvency work).

14.4 Non-regulated legal activities
There are many legal activities which are not regulated either by the Legal Services Act 2007 or by any other statute. You will be surprised to learn that many of the legal services an individual needs to use are in this regulatory desert.

A non-regulated legal activity may be offered by a regulated person such as a solicitor, barrister or legal executive. In which case the protections their regulators offer to consumers for regulated legal activities will also apply to these services as it is the *provider* who is regulated in all that they do.

Whereas, a non-regulated legal activity offered by a non-regulated person is simply unregulated and the consumer using this provider's services gains none of the protections which a regulated provider offers.

Non-regulated legal activities include:

*   Advice and representation at a police station
*   Assistance with non-contentious employment issues
*   Advice about mental health issues and detention
*   Will writing

It is most surprising that drafting a Will is not regulated. This is an area where many unregulated providers offer services which are potentially disastrous. Some providers of Will writing services may belong to a trade group which offers some form of protection to users of its members' services such as the Institute of Professional Will Writers https://www.ipw.org.uk or the Society of Will Writers https://www.willwriters.com. However, there is no obligation to belong to such a trade group and their ability to protect consumers, in the same way as say the Solicitors Regulation Authority, is limited.

Although there was strong debate about whether Will writing should be regulated at the time of the passage of the Legal Services Act 2007 it was not included. It was left to the Legal Services Board to consider whether it should use its powers at some point to make it a reserved legal activity.

The Competition and Markets Authority recommended in its report of December 2016 that the Ministry of Justice should undertake a review of the independence of regulators immediately and, in the longer term, review the entire system of regulation. However, in the Government's response to the CMA's report, only issued in December 2017, the Justice Minister Lord Keen of Elie QC said there will be no commitment to a formal review, instead he said that incremental change can bring about improvements. No doubt this lack of will to change the regulatory system is linked to the all-encompassing issue of the UK's exit from the European Union.

Lord Keen did say that the government accepted that it should review the case for extending redress to consumers using unauthorised providers of legal services. Currently, clients using such providers are unable to make any complaint to the Legal Ombudsman for redress whereas clients of regulated firms may do so when they have exhausted all a firm's internal complaints procedures.

14.5 The Solicitor's Code of Conduct

By way of an example, the regulation of solicitors and Alternative Business Structures is undertaken by the Solicitors Regulation Authority (SRA) which replaced *The Guide to the Professional Conduct of Solicitors* in 2007 with the Solicitors' Code of Conduct. This code appears only on the SRA's website and is updated regularly – the most recent version being the Solicitors' Code of Conduct 2011 – http://www.sra.org.uk/solicitors/handbook/code/content.page.

As the SRA state in their overview:

"The Code forms part of the Handbook, in which the 10 mandatory Principles are all-pervasive. They apply to all those we regulate and underpin all aspects of practice. They define the fundamental ethical and professional standards that we expect of all firms and individuals (including owners who may not be lawyers) when providing legal services. You should always have regard to the Principles and use them as your starting point when faced with an ethical dilemma.

Where two or more Principles come into conflict the one which takes precedence is the one which best serves the public interest in the particular circumstances, especially the public interest in the proper administration of justice. Compliance with the Principles is also subject to any overriding legal obligations."

A regulated entity must:

1. uphold the rule of law and the proper administration of justice;
2. act with integrity;
3. not allow your independence to be compromised;
4. act in the best interests of each client;
5. provide a proper standard of service to your clients;
6. behave in a way that maintains the trust the public places in you and in the provision of legal services;
7. comply with your legal and regulatory obligations and deal with your regulators and ombudsmen in an open, timely and co-operative manner;
8. run your business or carry out your role in the business effectively and in accordance with proper governance and sound financial and risk management principles;
9. run your business or carry out your role in the business in a way that encourages equality of opportunity and respect for diversity; and

10. protect client money and assets.

The Code is divided into five sections and focuses on the firm as follows:

- You and your client
- You and your business
- You and your regulator
- You and others
- Application, waivers and interpretation

Each section is divided into chapters dealing with particular regulatory issues, for example, client care, conflicts of interests, and publicity. These chapters show how the Principles apply in certain contexts through mandatory and non-mandatory provisions.

Some aspects of the Code are mandatory e.g. what are called 'Outcomes' and some parts of the Code are non-mandatory e.g. what are referred to as 'Indicative Behaviours'. From your point of view the first section of the Code (You and your client) is likely to be the most relevant and if there are mandatory Outcomes which the service offered should produce but which it did not, there might well be cause for complaint.

The purpose of the Indicative Behaviours is to provide some guidance as to what behaviour would be evidence of compliance with the stipulated Outcomes.

By way of an example, you may think there is unlikely to be a conflict of interest problem in a solicitor taking on a new Will client. This is not necessarily so. Clients who were married but then separate or get divorced represent a potential problem, particularly where they have re-married.

Each party to a marriage would have been a separate client (unless they made Mutual Wills possibly) and theoretically a firm can therefore act for either or both of them at any time subject to the rules on conflicts of interest and confidentiality.

a. Conflicts of interest
For solicitors it is necessary to consider as a first step whether the new parties on a re-marriage are likely to present conflicts

of interest and explain why it may be best for each person to be separately represented.

Obviously a solicitor must not act where a conflict of interest (or a significant risk of conflict) arises between two or more clients. Outcome 3.6 in the Code of Conduct says:

"Where there is a client conflict and the clients have a substantially common interest in relation to a matter or a particular aspect of it, you only act if:

(a) You have explained the relevant issues and risks to the clients and you have a reasonable belief that they understand those issues and risks;
(b) All the clients have given informed consent in writing to you acting;
(c) You are satisfied that it is reasonable for you to act for all the clients and that it is in their best interests; and
(d) You are satisfied that the benefits to the clients of you doing so outweigh the risks."

In a remarriage situation a solicitor should ensure that both parties to the new marriage sign separate Terms of Business when acting for them in preparing Wills. On its own this is not sufficient so the solicitor should provide an explanation as to how each person is entitled to separate representation should a conflict arise or risk that it could arise becomes apparent. Also, it may be prudent for the solicitor to obtain your informed consent in writing to acting on behalf of you both.

b. *Duty of confidentiality*

Principle 2 of Solicitors' Code of Conduct says that solicitors must act with integrity – so acting for one party to a marriage may in theory not be a conflict of interest but it does not sit well with a solicitor's duty to provide clients with the information they need to make informed decisions and the duty of confidentiality.

Chapter 4 of the Code of Conduct states in outcome 4.1:

"You must keep the affairs of clients confidential unless disclosure is required or permitted by law or the client consents."

For the purposes of Solicitors Code of Conduct 'Client' includes both a current client and a former client.

Outcome 4.2 says that any individual who is advising a client must make that client aware of all information material to that retainer of which the individual has personal knowledge and outcome 4.3 goes on to say that a solicitor must ensure that where his/her duty of confidentiality to one client comes into conflict with his/her duty of disclosure to another client, then the duty of confidentiality take precedence.

Practical problems inevitably arise where the wife, say, comes to instruct the firm to make a new Will and she attends the office with a third party such as a relative, friend or new 'man'. You would have to be careful not to disclose information about the ex-husband to the third party as you have a duty to keep that confidential and this continues even after the retainer with that client has ended.

If the original husband and wife were seen together and their Wills were prepared on the basis of this open discourse then there will not be confidential information obtained as between them since both were present in the discussion. This would mean that if say the wife subsequently asked the solicitor to change her Will following re-marriage he/she could in fact act for her since the information the solicitor had about the ex-husband would not be relevant confidential information that would stop the solicitor acting for the wife given she already knows this information. However, should the ex-husband subsequently ask you to change his Will you would not be able to do so because by then you would have relevant confidential information about the ex-wife which must remain confidential.

The intricacies of regulatory rules are sometimes hard to follow or apply to a particular situation and you may in fact need help from another lawyer to establish your rights under the regulatory framework, particularly whether you waived your rights at the time.

14.6 The Legal Ombudsman service

The Legal Ombudsman (LeO) service provides help to 'sort out complaints about the service you have received from your lawyer or claims management company in England and Wales.' The service is free, independent and fair. It does not extend to unregulated businesses.

The LeO service has a website at http://www.legalombudsman.org.uk where guidance is given about how to complain about a legal service provider and it even provides a template for a letter of complaint.

A complaint should first of all be made to the person indicated as responsible for handling complaints in the Terms of Business you signed with the regulated provider. In the case of a barrister, contact the barrister direct.

It is best to make your complaint in writing by letter or e-mail so that you can keep a copy and there is less opportunity for mis-understanding. Use a simple bring forward reminder to check whether you have received an acknowledgement or reply after, say, seven days. If not, you should follow up in case for some reason your letter or e-mail has not reached them.

The LeO cannot help if you have not made a complaint to the service provider first. Only if they have not provided a response within eight weeks can you refer the matter to the LeO for help. Equally, if your complaint starts a dialogue with your legal provider but ultimately you do not feel they have provided a satisfactory outcome for you then you can complain to the LeO.

The LeO's factsheet on how to complain says:

"Ordinarily, you can ask us to look at your complaint if it meets all three of the steps below:

1. The problem or when you found out about it, happened after 5 October 2010; and
2. You are referring your complaint to the Legal Ombudsman within either of the following:
    o   Six years of the problem happening; or
    o   Three years from when you found out about it; and
3. You are referring your complaint to us within six months of your service provider's final response.

If your complaint does not meet these time limits we may not be able to investigate it."

Websites mentioned

Chapter 1 -
1. UK Government Website https://www.gov.uk
2. Royal Institute of Chartered Surveyors list of conveyancers https://www.localbuildingsurveyor.co.uk
3. Really Moving https://www.reallymoving.com
4. The Law Society https://www.lawsociety.org.uk

Chapter 2 -
5. The Family Mediation Council https://www.familymediation council.org.uk
6. Family Law Partners https://www.gov.uk/check-legal-aid
7. Money Advice Service https://www.moneyadviceservice.org. uk
8. Royal College of Psychiatrists http://www.rcpsych.ac.uk
9. Sheppersons Solicitors https://www.sheppersonssolicitors. com
10. Blake Morgan https://www.blakemorgan.co.uk
11. Resolution http://www.resolution.org.uk

Chapter 3 – What you need to know to get the best out of lawyers who help you to make a Will
12. Citizen's Advice Bureau https://www.citizensadvice.org.uk
13. Moore Probate Research – http://mprmissingheirs.co.uk
14. Title Research – https://www.titleresearch.com/our-services
15. Estate Research – https://www.estateresearch.co.uk/missing-beneficiaries
16. Finders – http://www.findersinternational.co.uk
17. Title Research https://www.titleresearch.com
18. The Gazette https://www.thegazette.co.uk/all-notices/content/101190
19. Lawskills https://www.lawskills.co.uk

Chapter 4 – What you need to know to get the best out of lawyers who help manage someone's finances
20. Solicitors for the Elderly – see http://www.sfe.legal
21. The Society of Trusts and Estates (www.step.org)
22. Scotland Public Guardian – http://www.publicguardian-scotland.gov.uk
23. Northern Ireland Law Society – https://www.lawsoc-ni.org

24. Action on Elder Abuse – https://www.elderabuse.org.uk/ financial

Chapter 5 – Is price all you should be concerned with?
25. Competition and Markets Authority – Legal Services Market Study – https://www.gov.uk/cma-cases/legal-services-market-study
26. Executor Solutions – http://www.executorsolutions.co.uk

Chapter 6 – What you need to know to get the best out of lawyers who help you to administer someone's estate on death
27. NHS – Bereavement https://www.nhs.uk/Livewell/bereavement
28. Counselling directory – http://www.counselling-directory.org.uk/bereavement.html
29. Executor Solutions – http://www.executorsolutions.co.uk
30. London Gazette https://www.thegazette.co.uk/wills-and-probate/place-a-deceased-estates-notice
31. ICAEW – https://www.icaew.com
32. the Association of Certified Accountants – http://www.accaglobal.com/uk
33. National Will Register – https://www.nationalwillregister.co.uk

Chapter 7 – What you need to know to get the best out of lawyers who help you to mitigate tax on death
34. Money Advice Service – https://www.moneyadviceservice.org.uk

Chapter 8 – What you need to know to get the best out of lawyers who help you to plan the succession to your business
35. Deloitte – https://www2.deloitte.com
36. Price Waterhouse Coopers PwC – https://www.pwc.com
37. Gannons – http://www.gannons.co.uk
38. Lupton Fawcett – https://social.luptonfawcett.com
39. Confederation of British Industry (CBI) see http://www.cbi.org.uk
40. Institute of Directors – https://www.iod.com
41. Chambers of Commerce – http://www.britishchambers.org.uk

42. Josiah Hincks - https://www.josiahhincks.co.uk
43. The Telegraph - http://www.telegraph.co.uk
44. FindLaw - http://smallbusiness.findlaw.com

Chapter 9 - What you need to know to get the best out of lawyers who help you to understand your family trust

Chapter 10 - What you need to know about the costs of care and how to help your lawyer advise you

45. Age UK - https://www.ageuk.org.uk
46. Society of Later Life Advisers - https://societyoflaterlife advisers.co.uk

Chapter 11 - What you need to know about public bodies who may be able to help you

47. http://adlib.everysite.co.uk/adlib/defra/content.aspx?id=00 0IL3890W.16NTBYC4N021T4
48. OFSTED - http://www.ofsted.gov.uk
49. Charity Commission - https://www.gov.uk/government/ organisations/charity-commission
50. Parliamentary & Health Ombudsman - http://www. ombudsman.org.uk

Chapter 12 - How law is made

51. BAILII - http://www.bailii.org
52. HMSO - http://www.hmso.gov.uk
53. UK Legislation - http://www.legislation.gov.uk
54. Houses of Parliament - http://www.parliament.uk
55. Delia Venables Legal Resources, UK and Ireland - http:// www.venables.co.uk

Chapter 13 - Where lawyers fit into the English legal system

56. Bar Standards Board - https://www.barstandardsboard.org. uk
57. Bar Council - http://www.barcouncil.org.uk
58. National Association of Licensed Paralegals - http://www. nationalparalegals.co.uk
59. The University of Law - http://www.law.ac.uk
60. Legal Choices - http://www.legalchoices.org.uk/legal-choices
61. Law Society of Scotland - https://www.lawscot.org.uk
62. Advocates in Scotland - http://www.advocates.org.uk
63. Law Society of Northern Ireland - https://www.lawsoc-ni.org

64. Bar of Northern Ireland – http://www.barofni.com

Chapter 14 – The Regulatory Framework
65. Institute of Professional Will Writers – https://www.ipw.org.uk
66. Society of Will Writers – https://www.willwriters.com
67. SRA's Solicitors Code of Conduct – http://www.sra.org.uk/solicitors/handbook/code/content.page
68. The Legal Ombudsman – http://www.legalombudsman.org.uk

The Street-wise Patient's Guide To Surviving Cancer

How to be an active, organised, informed, and welcomed patient.

Karol Sikora

About this book

How to survive, and live with, cancer.
* Short, sharp practical guide.
* Shows patients how to take control of their care.
* How to get the system to work for you.
* Gives 100 advisory websites, with expert notes.
* Absolutely up-to-date.

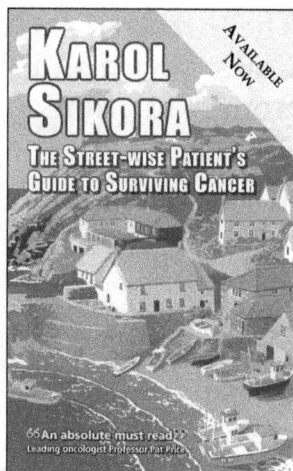

About the author

Professor Karol Sikora, MA PhD FRCR FRCP FFPM is an internationally-famous cancer doctor. Former Chief, World Health Organisation Cancer Programme.

Reviews

"This book is about what the NHS doesn't tell you but what as a cancer patient you need to know. It is also a fascinating autobiography and medical history by one of the most famous cancer specialists in the country."
        – **Professor Angus Dalgleish**, *St. George's Hospital*, London

"At last a reliable source of impartial advice which will empower patients to take control of their cancer treatment. The more patients understand the more they can take back control, get the best treatment for their cancer and move positively on. This book is just what we need. All patients should read it, understand their cancer and what they can do to help themselves."
        – **Professor Pat Price**, *Christie Hospital*, Manchester

"It perfectly fulfils its purpose. And what a mind, what a man, what an authority Sikora is!"
        – **Professor John Vincent**

The cover illustration is by the artist Brian Sweet, reproduced courtesy of Yellow House Art Licensing, www.yellowhouseartlicensing.com

The Street-wise Guide to Coping with and Recovering from Addiction

Dr. Robert Lefever

ROBERT LEFEVER

THE STREET-WISE GUIDE TO COPING WITH AND RECOVERING FROM ADDICTION

66 No one has ever written better about addiction.99
– Jeffrey Robinson

About this book

Everyone 'knows' what addiction is and what should be done for it. But as this book shows, individual experience cannot apply universally. The psychology of denial – addicts telling themselves that they aren't addicted – is the most devastating feature of addiction.

This book offers much practical guidance, with reference to entirely anonymised individual experiences. The entire emphasis of the book is on what works. It also explains why some approaches do not work.

The author contends that there are three causes for addiction: the antecedent cause is probably genetic; the contributory cause is emotional, physical or social trauma leading to a craving for mood-alteration; the precipitant cause is exposure – discovering something that lifts our mood. Treatment, he believes, will therefore also have to be in three phases, in reverse order: abstinence; emotional (not intellectual) therapy; daily relapse prevention by working the Twelve Step Programme first formulated by Alcoholics Anonymous.

Dr Lefever explains specific addictions. These come in three clusters: hedonistic, nurturant and relationship. Some addicts have just one of these clusters, some two, some all. He shows how patients and their families can take action to unblock delay in seeking recovery. He considers known intervention techniques and family work in tackling compulsive helping, where pain is the great teacher.

This practical book, which also explains the key terminology used in the field, offers important guidance on life in recovery, on real friendships, on spontaneity, creativity and enthusiasm.

Dr Lefever also examines the future of addiction treatment, as well as its politics.

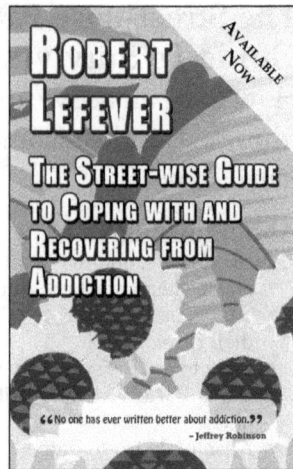

The Street-wise Guide to Getting the Best Mental Health Care

How to Survive the Mental Health System and Get Some Proper Help

Dr Raj Persaud and Dr Peter Bruggen

About this book

Never before has a guide on how to negotiate the increasingly stretched NHS, and obtain the care you need, been more essential.

This offers crucial advice to families and to individuals on how to not be palmed off with inadequate care.

And how to grasp what you are entitled to - as well as how to best look after the well-being of yourself and your loved ones.

This radical new and expert book shows you:
- how to diagnose yourself
- how to develop a better understanding of what to do about the most common mental health problems
- how to engage and negotiate with GP and specialist services.
- how to know when you need to get professional help, and the issues you can effectively and safely tackle yourself.

The book is essential in enabling you or your supporters to get the system to change your diagnosis if you are not happy with it.
The authors of this new guide are both internationally-known Consultant Psychiatrists with many decades of experience of working on frontline psychiatric services.

They show you how to:
- get your problems or those of a relative treated with adequate priority.
- to see the records kept on you.
- to evaluate if you are getting the correct treatment.
- to find out if that mortgage you got denied was down to something a doctor recorded in your medical history.
- to correct your physician's notes if they are wrong.
- to obtain the best specialist help available in the NHS.

Various theories are commonly advanced as to the dramatic increase in poor mental health across broad swathes of our community, with tough economic conditions and social media frequently blamed. None of these problems are going to go away soon.
This book is your essential guide to getting the best care in the prevailing critical situation.

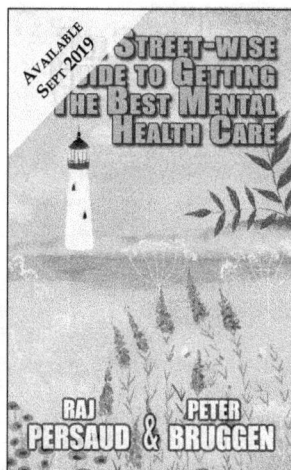

The Street-wise Guide to Surviving a Stroke

Tom Balchin

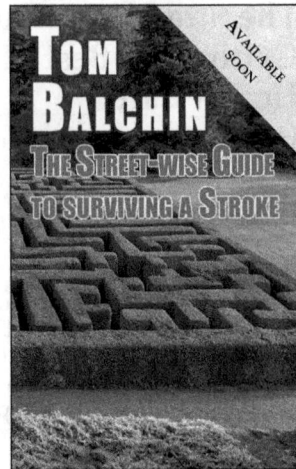

About this book

This concise and practical book is a 'how-to' in the truest sense of the word - it charts a path through the maze for you and enables you quickly to become the expert-patient.

The Street-wise guide offers you real-life options for real self-recovery and self-management of the physical limitations caused by stroke.

The author is himself a stroke survivor who has created, over the last twenty years, an internationally-known new approach to innovative stroke rehabilitation.

Every stroke results in different outcomes, dependent on thousands of variables. A clear-cut background to stroke and the problems it may cause is presented here.

Here you will learn:

- Why your own stroke has caused physical and psychological limitations.
- How to regain action control and self-manage using evidence-based and innovative strategies.
- How to take advantage of your brain's capacity for neuroplasticity by learning how to dramatically extend the 'therapeutic time window' you may be told about.

Dr. Balchin reveals how best to recover lower and upper limb action control as well as strength and cardiovascular health via the introduction of a special re-training programme that you can adopt, adapt and explore further to your own requirements.

He shows you how to transition to successful 'life after stroke' - whatever is your ultimate goal. This may be about enhancing your quality of life and coping abilities or seeking ultimately to get back to work. Dr. Balchin shows here how novel home-use and clinically-based tools based on technologies to improve motor recovery can work. The reader is offered key information on robotic devices, and on brain computer interfaces, as well as virtual reality and non-invasive brain stimulation.

Dr. Balchin explains the drugs that stroke survivors are prescribed and what they do, how to access further direct clinical and community sources and what you need to know of the availability of further cutting-edge interventions on the horizon.

The book will be of major assistance to anyone who has had the misfortune to have had a stroke and is entering the recovery phase, and to their families and supporters. The text is written for stroke survivors, but it has considerable relevance to those with other neurologically disabling conditions, such as acquired brain injury or spinal injury.

Most importantly, this book will help you to show those who care about you most that you can do it. You can beat stroke!

www.ingramcontent.com/pod-product-compliance
Lightning Source LLC
Chambersburg PA
CBHW061213220326
41599CB00025B/4622